Felix Mendelssohn

MAJOR ORCHESTRAL WORKS

Felix Mendelssohn

MAJOR ORCHESTRAL WORKS

A Midsummer Night's Dream (complete)

The Hebrides Overture (Fingal's Cave)

Calm Sea and Prosperous Voyage Overture

Symphony No. 3 in A ("Scottish")

Symphony No. 4 in A ("Italian")

From the Breitkopf & Härtel Complete Works Edition

Edited by Julius Rietz

Dover Publications, Inc., New York

Published in Canada by General Publishing Company, Ltd., 30 Lesmill Road, Don Mills, Toronto, Ontario.

Published in the United Kingdom by Constable and Company, Ltd., 10 Orange Street, London WC 2.

This Dover edition, first published in 1975, is an unabridged republication of the following sections from *Felix Mendelssohn Bartholdy's Werke. Kritisch durchgesehene Ausgabe von Julius Rietz. Mit Genehmigung der Originalverleger*, originally published by Breitkopf & Härtel, Leipzig, between 1874 and 1877:

Serie 15, Grössere weltliche Gesangwerke. No. 117, Musik zu Sommernachtstraum von Shakespeare, Op. 61.

Serie 2, Ouverturen für Orchester. No. 8, Ouverture zu den Hebriden (Fingals-Höhle), Op. 26. No. 9, Ouverture Meeresstille und glückliche Fahrt, Op. 27.

Serie 1, Symphonien für Orchester. No. 3, Dritte (schottische) Symphonie, Op. 56. No. 4, Vierte (italienische) Symphonie, Op. 90.

International Standard Book Number: 0-486-23184-4
Library of Congress Catalog Card Number: 75-2936

Manufactured in the United States of America
Dover Publications, Inc.
180 Varick Street
New York, N.Y. 10014

Contents

Overture and Incidental Music to *A Midsummer Night's Dream* by Shakespeare Opp. 21 & 61

OUVERTURE.

Allegro di molto.

Flauto I.
Flauto II.
Oboe I.
Oboe II.
Clarinetto I in A.
Clarinetto II in A.
Fagotto I.
Fagotto II.
Corni in E.
Trombe in E.
Ophicleïde.
Timpani in E.H.
Violino I. (divisi) — sempre stacc.
Violino II. (divisi) — sempre stacc.
Viola.
Violoncello.
Basso.

Allegro di molto.

pizz.

p

pp

stacc.

pp

stacc.

pp

pizz.

arco

pizz.

pp

pp

pp

pp

pp

pp

pp

pp

pizz.

pizz.

arco

pp pp pp pp pp pp pp pp pp pp pp

A
ff
tr
arco
A

Viol.I.

Viol.II.

ff
sf
f

f
f
f
f
f
f
cresc.
ff
cresc.
ff
cresc.
ff
cresc.
ff
cresc.
ff

f
f
cresc.
f
f
cresc.
cresc.
cresc.
cresc.
f
cresc.
f
f
f
ff
cresc.
cresc.
cresc.
cresc.
cresc.

B
ff
p
sf
pp
pizz.
tr

p
pp
arco

pp

pp

p

p

p

p

p

p

p

p

p

p

p

p

divisi

p

p

p

arco

p

p

f
mf
p
cresc.
dolce
pizz.

mf
cresc.
f
pp
più f
p
arco

C
ff
f
cresc.
a.2.
C

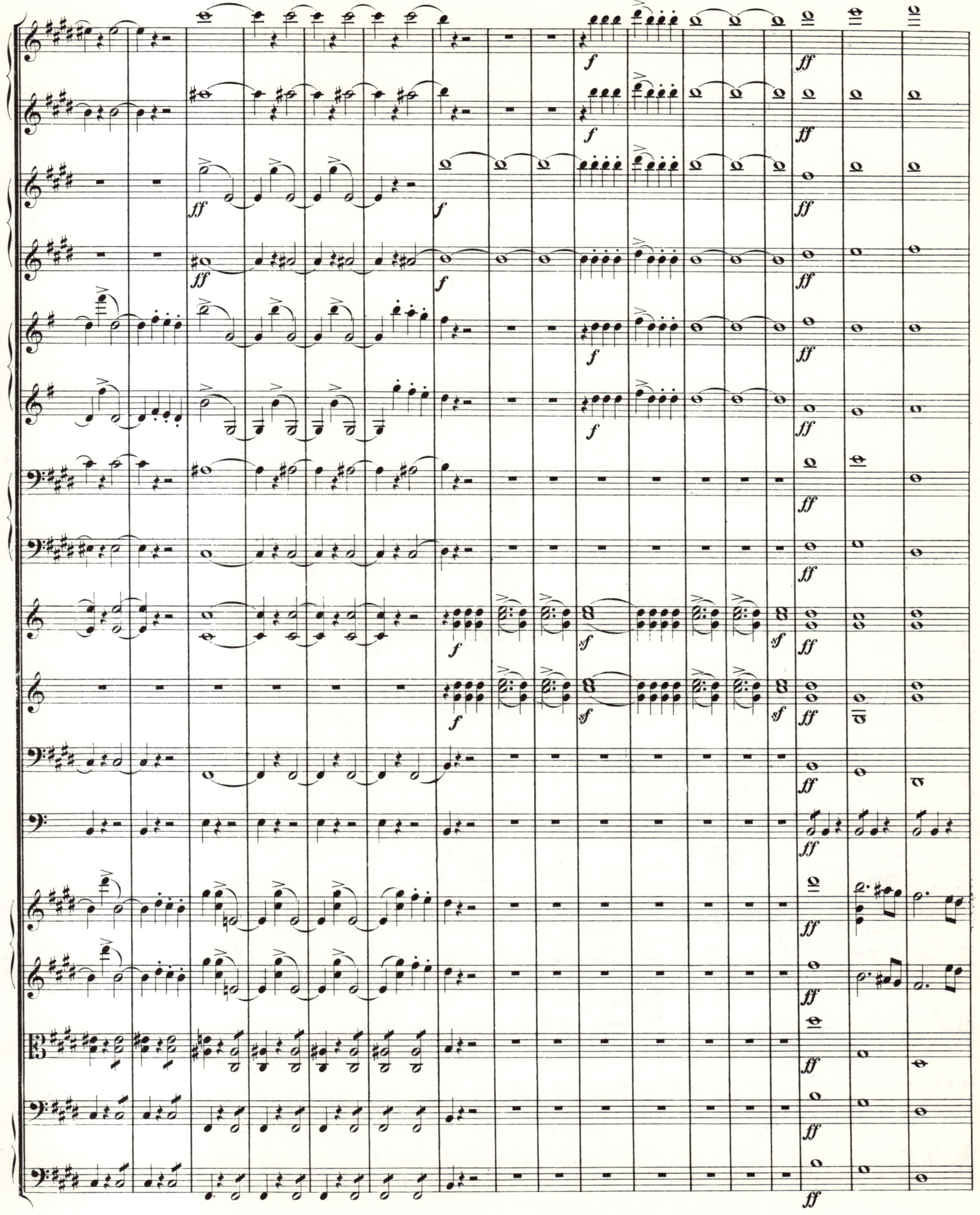
f
ff
sf

a.2.

D

ff ff ff ff ff ff ff ff ff ff ff ff

p

ff divisi ff pp stacc. pp stacc.

divisi ff ff pp stacc. pp stacc.

ff ff ff

D

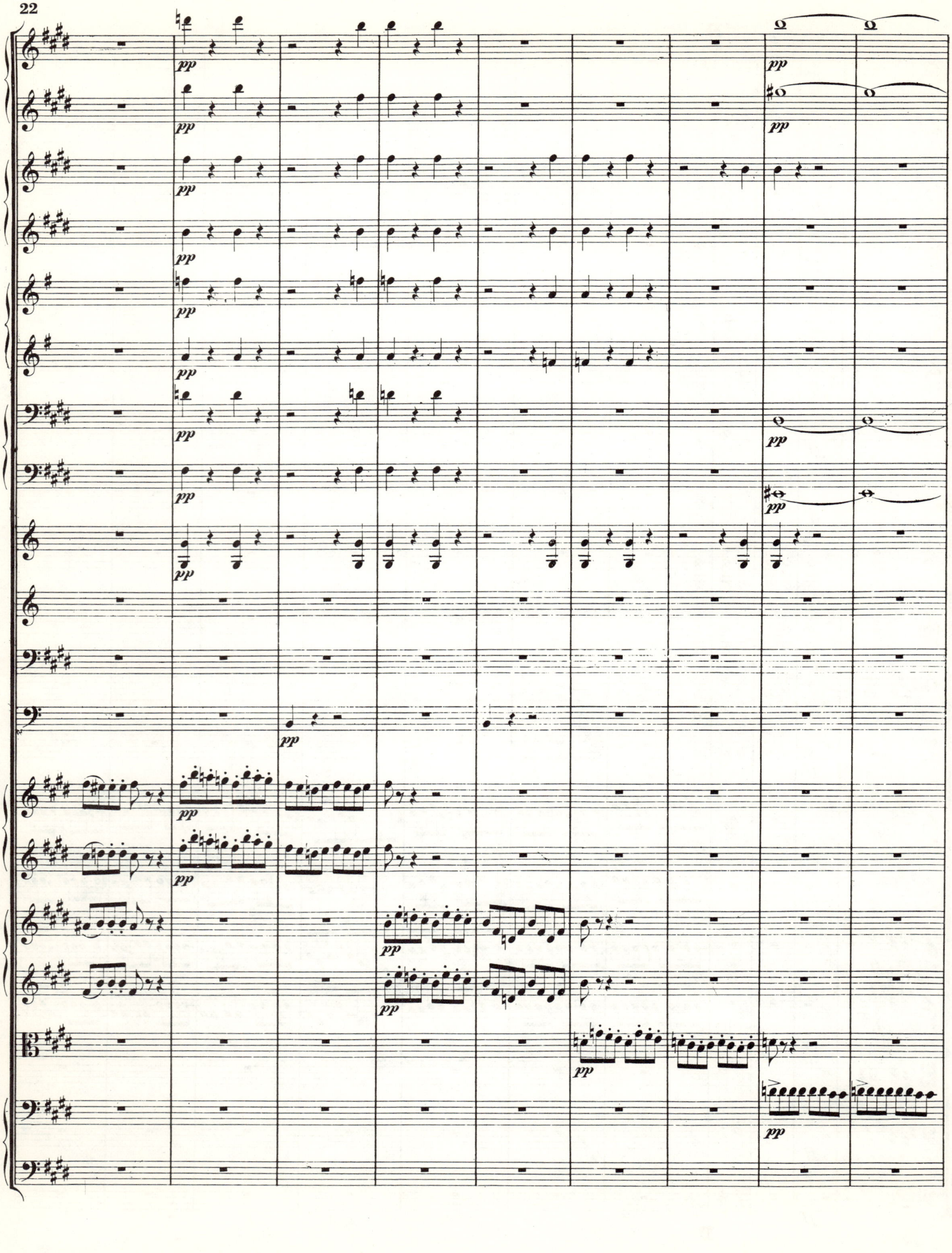
pp

pp

pp

pp

pp

pp

pp

pp

uno Violoncello
uno Basso

a 2.
Viol. I.
Viol. II.
Tutti.
Tutti.
pp

pp
pp
pp
pp
pp
pp
con tutta la forza
a 2.
ff
dim.
poco a poco
pp
dim.
poco a poco
tr
pp
tr
pp
pp
pp
pp
pp
divisi
pp
pp
sempre pp
pp
pp

E
pp
pp
pp
pp
pp
pp
pp
pp
tr
ff
dim.
pp
pp
tr
pp
pp
pp
pp
pp
pp
pp
pp
pp
pp
pp
pp
pp
E

a 2.
p
dim.
pp
p

a 2.

pp

pp

divisi

pizz.

pp

pizz.

pp pp pp pp pp pp pp pp pp pp pp pp pp pp pp pp pp pp pp

arco pizz. arco pizz. pizz. pp pp

F

pp

pp

pp

pp

pp

pp

pp

pp

pp

arco

arco

pp

arco

F

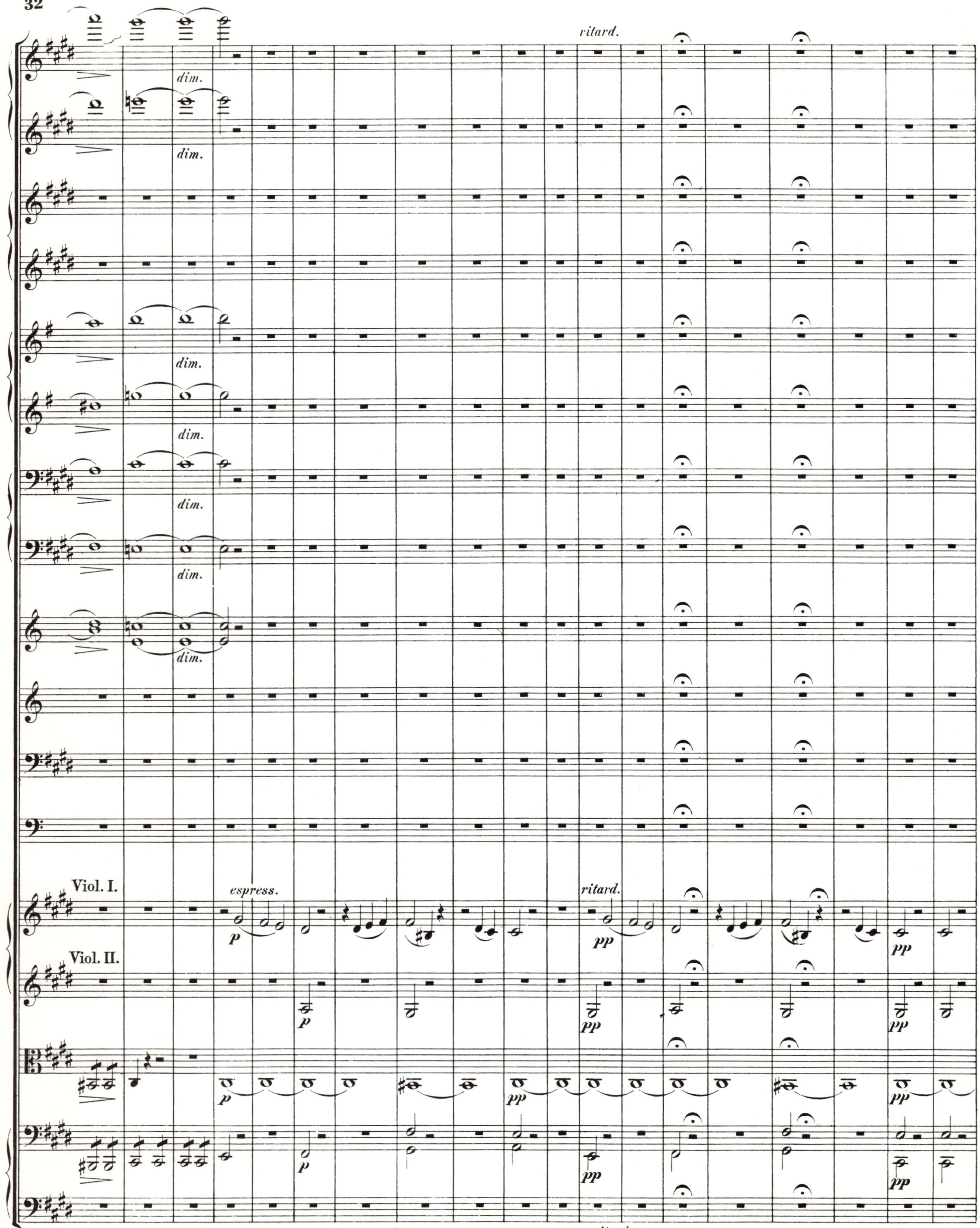
ritard.
dim.
dim.
dim.
dim.
dim.
dim.
dim.
Viol. I.
espress.
p
ritard.
pp
pp
Viol. II.
p
pp
pp
p
pp
pp
p
pp
pp
ritard.

Tempo I.

p pp p pp p pp p pp p pp p pp p pp p pp p pp p p

divisi

pp pp pp pp pp pp pp pp

divisi

pizz.

p

mf

p

p

p

pizz.

pp
pp
pp
pp
pp
p
tr
arco
pizz.
pizz.

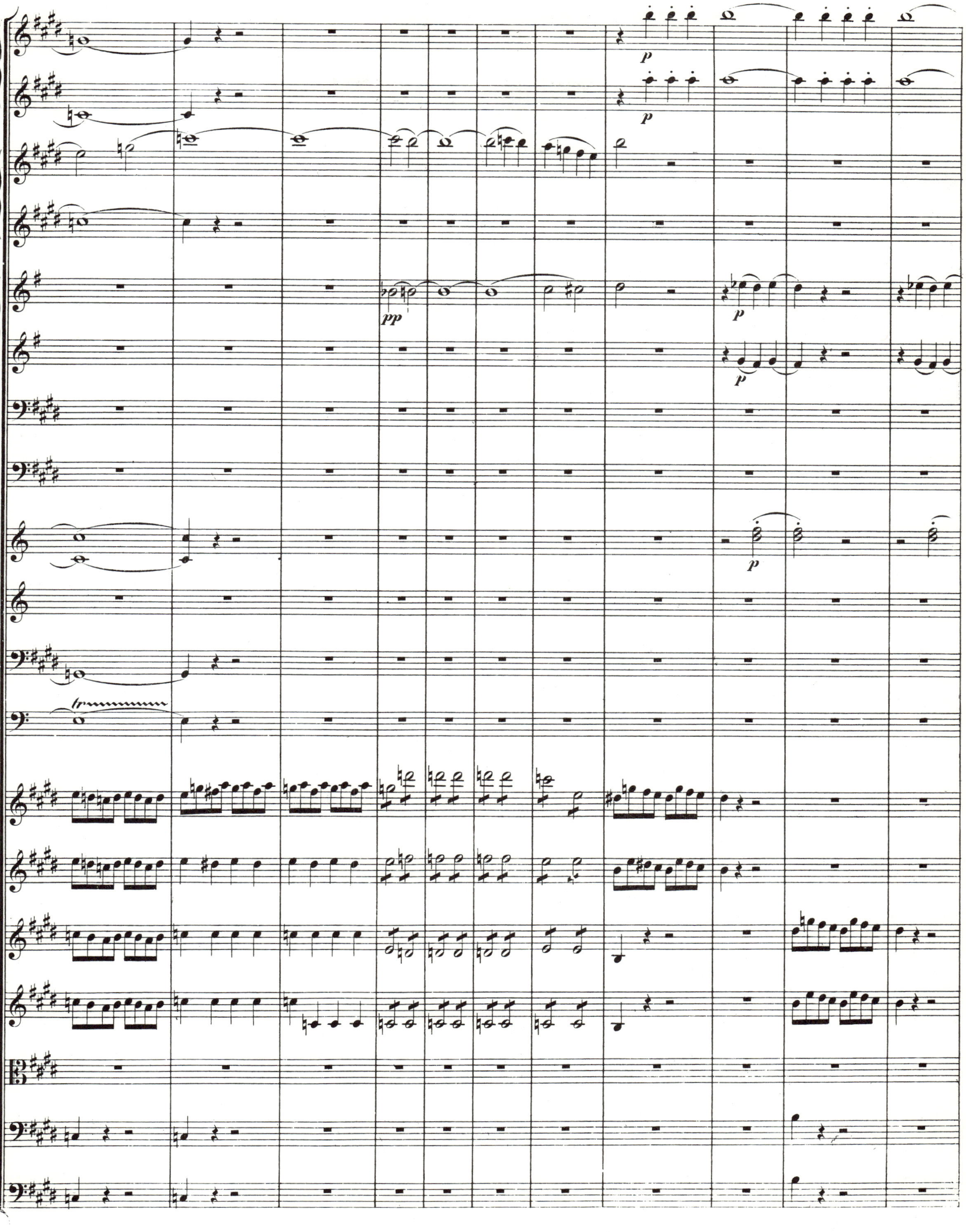

Viol. I.
pp
Viol. II.
arco
pp
p
arco
p

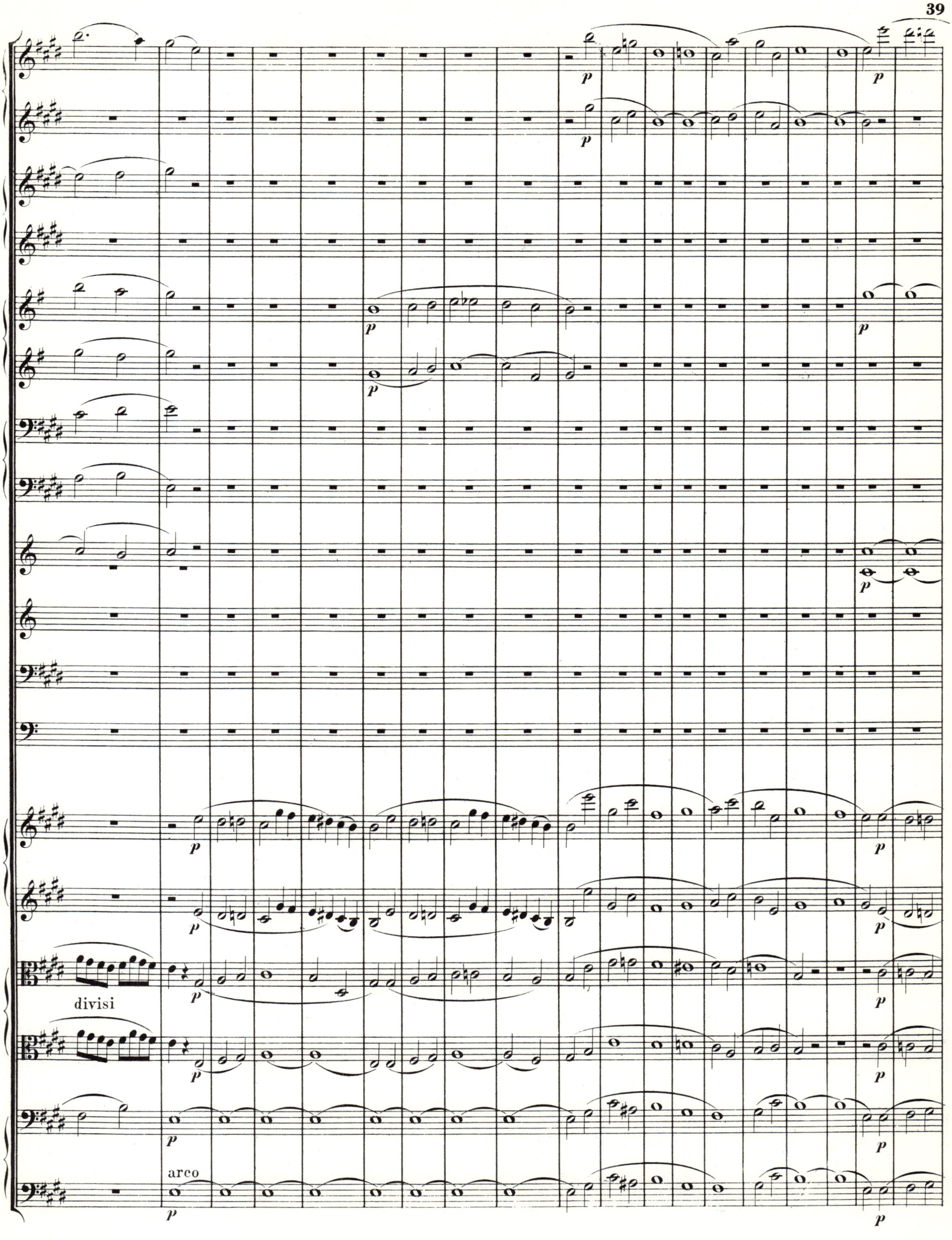

divisi

arco

cresc.
p
f
mf
sf cresc.

f f f f f f f f

mf cresc. mf cresc. mf cresc. mf cresc.

mf pp cresc. mf cresc.

mf mf mf

cresc. mf cresc.

p cresc. mf cresc.

cresc. mf cresc.

p cresc. mf cresc.

p cresc. mf cresc.

G
ff
f
cresc.
più f
G

f
f
f
f
f
f
f
f
f

ff
ff
ff
ff
ff
ff
ff
ff
ff
ff
ff
ff
ff
ff
ff
f
f
f
f
f
f
f
f
f
f
a 2.
f
f
tr
f

sf
f
sf
tr
f

f sempre
f
sf
a 2.
tr
sempre

f
sf
ff
a 2.
tr

sf
ff
a 2.
tr
f

a.2.

H

ff sf

con tutta la forza

divisi

pp

H

p

pp

pp

pp

pp

pp

divisi

pp

pp pp pp pp pp pp pp pp pp pp

I
K
Poco ritenuto
dim.
dim.
dim.
pp
dim.
pp
dolce
pp
pp
Poco ritenuto
dim.
pp
pp
Viol.I.
Poco ritenuto
pp
Viol.II.
pp
pizz.
pizz.
I
K Poco ritenuto

ritard.

p pp

p pp

p pp

p pp

pp dolce

p pp

pp

p pp

dolce

ritard.

pp

pp

tr

pp

ritard.

pp

pp

pp

pp

pp

arco

pp

pp

arco

pp

pp ritard.

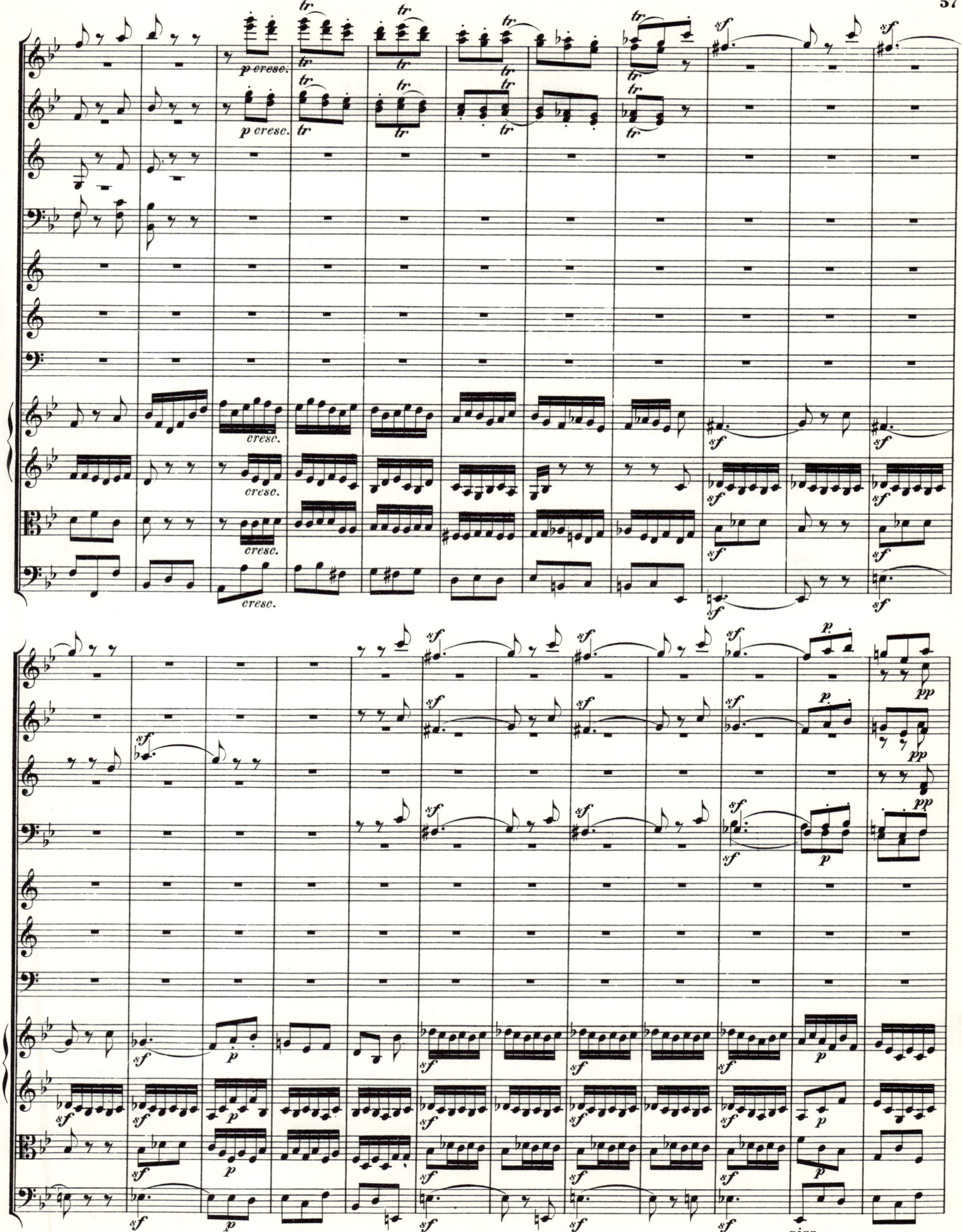

tr
p cresc.
cresc.
sf
p
pp
pizz.

pp
arco
p

cresc.
dim.
al
pp
p
a 2.
p
cresc.
arco

p cresc.
f
cresc.
ff
sf
dim.
pizz.
arco
pp

cresc.
a 2.
tr
pizz.
dim.
divisi
arco

a 2.
cresc.
f
sf
ff
arco
p
in C.
tr
sempre ff

dim.
dim.
dim.
dim.
p
dim.
p
dim.
dim.
p
dim.
dim.
p
dim.
divisi
p
dim.
pp
pp
pp
pp
pp
pp
pizz.
pp
dim.
pizz.
p
p
p
p
p
arco
p
pizz.

Vcl.
Basso
pizz.
arco
dim.
pizz.
Bassi
in D.

arco
pp
p
pp sempre
pp
pp
sf
sf
sf
sf
dim.
dim.
pp
Basso
Vcl.

p
p
p
pizz.
Bassi
pp
a 2.
p
in C.
p

cresc.
cresc.
a 2.
a 2.
arco
cresc.
cresc.
cresc.
tr

a 2.
a 2.
in C.
pp
pp
p
p
p
p
Vcl.
Basso
pizz.
p
p
p
p

cresc.
f
p
sf
dim.
Bassi
arco

sempre staccato
pp
pizz.
p
sempre più
sempre più pp
sempre stacc.

cresc.
dim.
pp
pizz.
arco
Vorhang auf.
The curtain is drawn.
Puck. He Geist! Wo geht die Reise hin? attacca
Puck. How now, spirit! whither wander you?

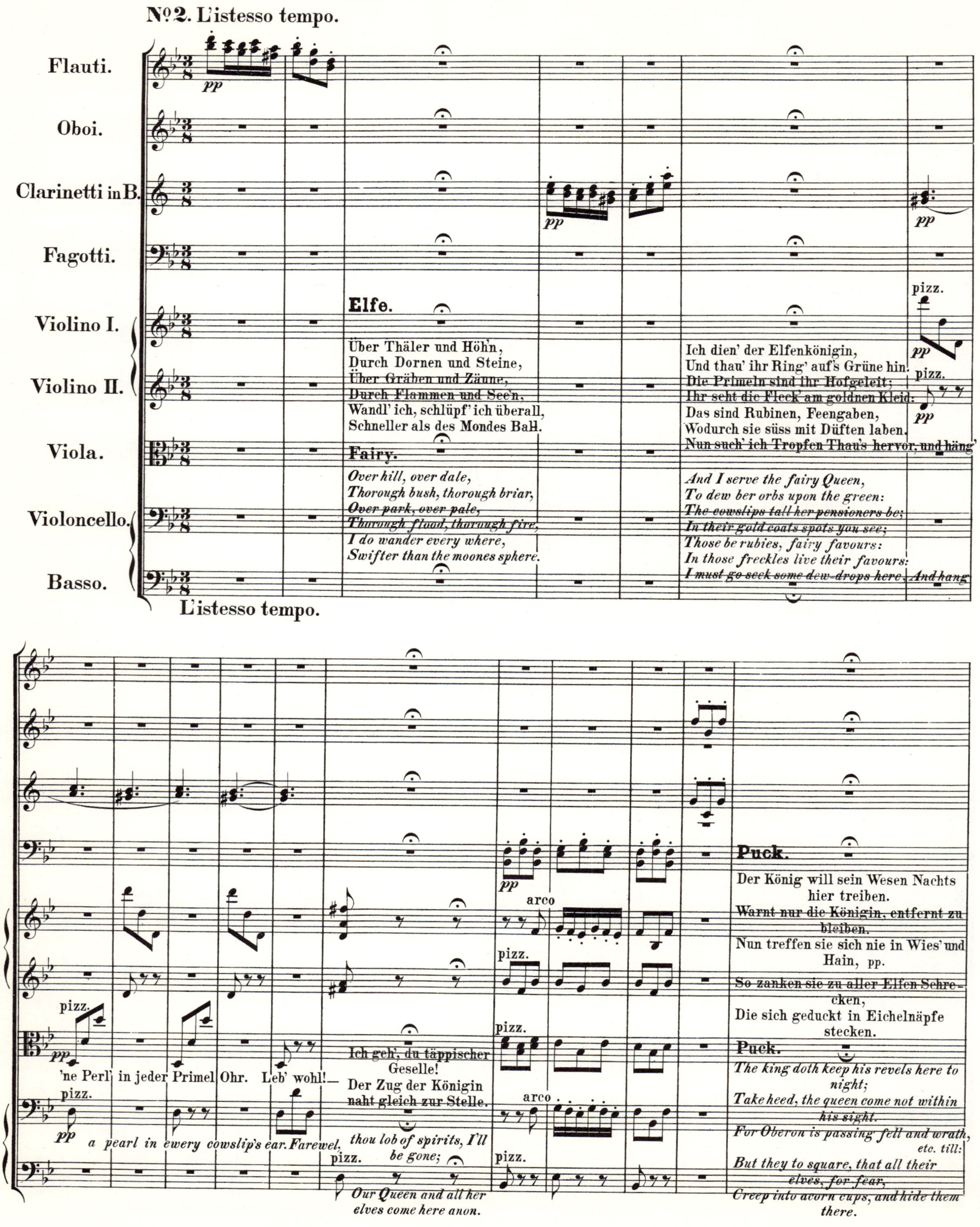

No 2. L'istesso tempo.

Flauti.
Oboi.
Clarinetti in B.
Fagotti.
Violino I.
Violino II.
Viola.
Violoncello.
Basso.

pp

Elfe.

Über Thäler und Höh'n,
Durch Dornen und Steine,
Über Gräben und Zäune,
Durch Flammen und See'n,
Wandl' ich, schlüpf' ich überall,
Schneller als des Mondes Ball.

Fairy.

Over hill, over dale,
Thorough bush, thorough briar,
Over park, over pale,
Thorough flood, thorough fire,
I do wander every where,
Swifter than the moones sphere.

Ich dien' der Elfenkönigin,
Und thau' ihr Ring' auf's Grüne hin.
Die Primeln sind ihr Hofgeleit;
Ihr seht die Fleck' am goldnen Kleid:
Das sind Rubinen, Feengaben,
Wodurch sie süss mit Düften laben.
Nun such' ich Tropfen Thau's hervor, und häng'

And I serve the fairy Queen,
To dew her orbs upon the green:
The cowslips tall her pensioners be;
In their gold coats spots you see;
Those be rubies, fairy favours:
In those freckles live their favours:
I must go seek some dew-drops here, And hang

pizz. pp

L'istesso tempo.

pizz. pp arco

'ne Perl' in jeder Primel Ohr. Leb' wohl! —

a pearl in ewery cowslip's ear. Farewel,

Ich geh', du täppischer Geselle!
Der Zug der Königin naht gleich zur Stelle.

thou lob of spirits, I'll be gone;
Our Queen and all her elves come here anon.

Puck.

Der König will sein Wesen Nachts hier treiben.
Warnt nur die Königin, entfernt zu bleiben.
Nun treffen sie sich nie in Wies' und Hain, pp.
So zanken sie zu aller Elfen Schrecken,
Die sich geduckt in Eichelnäpfe stecken.

Puck.

The king doth keep his revels here to night;
Take heed, the queen come not within his sight.
For Oberon is passing fell and wrath,
etc. till:
But they to square, that all their elves, for fear,
Creep into acorn cups, and hide them there.

cresc.
Elfe.
Wenn du nicht ganz dich zu verstellen weisst,
So bist du jener schlaue Poltergeist pp. bis:
Doch wer dich freundlich grüsst, dir Liebes thut,
Dem hilfst du gern, und ihm gelingt es gut.
Bist du der Kobold nicht?
Fairy.
Either I mistake your shape and making quite,
Or else you are that shrewd and knavish sprite, etc. till:
Those that Hobgoblin call you, and sweet Puck,
You do their work, and they shall have good luck:
Are not you he?
Puck.
Du hast's gerathen,
Ich schwärme Nachts umher auf solche Thaten.
Oft lacht bei meinen Scherzen Oberon pp. bis:
Ich gleit' ihr weg, sie setzt zur Erde sich auf ihren Steiss,
und schreit: Perdauz! und hustet pp.
Puck.
Thou speak'st aright,
I am that merry wanderer of the night.
I jest to Oberon, and make him smile etc. till:
Then slip I from her bum, down topples she,
And tailor cries, and falls into a cough. etc.
dim.
Dialog geht fort bis:
Mach' Platz nun, Elfchen, hier kommt Oberon.
Elfe.
Hier meine Königin. O macht' er sich davon!
Dialogue continues till:
But room, Fairy, here comes Oberon.
Fairy.
And here my mistress. — 'Would that he were gone!

Allegro vivace.

Flauti.
Oboi.
Clarinetti in A.
Fagotti.
Corni in E.
Trombe in C.
Triangolo.
Piatti.
Violino I.
Violino II.
Viola.
Violoncello e Basso.

(Die Elfen erscheinen in zwei Zügen.)

(Oberon with his train and Titania with hers enter at opposite sides.)

Allegro vivace.

a 2.

a 2.

cresc.
pizz.
arco
divisi
p
dim.
sf

cresc.
dim.
Oberon.
Schlimm treffen wir bei Mondenlicht, Du stolze Titania! pp.
Dialog.
Oberon.
Ill meet by moonlight, proud Titania. etc.
arco
Oberon.
Wie lange denkt ihr hier im Hain zu weilen?
Titania.
Vielleicht bis nach des Theseus Hochzeitfest. pp. bis:
Titania.
Nicht um dein Königreich! Ihr Elfen fort mit mir; denn Zank erhebt sich, weil' ich länger hier.
Oberon.
How long within this wood intend you stay?
Titania.
Perchance, till after Theseus' wedding day etc. till:
Not for thy kingdom. _ Fairies, away!
Who shall chide down-right, if I longer stay.
Trombe tacent
(Titania mit ihrem Gefolge ab.)
(Exeunt Titania and her train.)

dim.
pp
Timpani in D. A.
cresc.
Oberon.
Gut, zieh' nur hin! pp. bis:
Puck.
Rund um die Erde zieh' ich einen Gürtel
in viermal zehn Minuten.
Ob.
Well, go thy way! etc. till:
Puck.
I'll put a girdle round about the earth
In forty minutes.
(Puck ab.)
(Exit Puck.)
pizz.
arco
ff
Oberon.
Hab' ich nur den Saft erst, pp. bis:
(Demetrius und Helena ab.)
Oberon.
Geh', Nymphe, nur! Er soll uns nicht von hinnen,
Bis du ihn fliehst, und er dich will gewinnen.
Ob.
Having once this juice, etc. till:
(Exit Demetrius and Helena.)
Ob.
Fare thee well, nymph! ere he do leave this grove,
Thou shalt fly him, and he shall seek thy love.
(Puck zurück.)
(Re-enter Puck.)
Oberon. Hast du die Blume pp. bis: Puck. Verlasst euch, Herr, auf eures Knechtes Treu'. (Beide ab.)
Oberon. Hast thou the flower etc. till: Puck. Fear not, my lord, your servant shall do so. (Exeunt.)
attacca

No. 3. LIED mit CHOR. _ SONG with CHORUS.
Allegro ma non troppo.
Flauti.
Oboi.
Clarinetti in A.
Fagotti.
Corni in D.
Trombe in D.
Timpani in D.A.
Violino I.
Violino II.
Viola.
con sordino
pizz.
pp
Titania.
Kommt, einen Ringel-, einen Feensang,
Dann auf das Drittel 'ner Minute fort!
Soprano I Solo.
Erster Elfe.
First Fairy.
Soprano II Solo.
Zweiter Elfe.
Second Fairy.
Come, now a roundel, and a fairy song!
Then, for the third part of a minute, hence!
Chor der Elfen.
Chorus of Fairies.
Soprano I.
Soprano II.
Alto I.
Alto II.
Violoncello e Basso.
Allegro ma non troppo.

pp
dimin.
pp
Fl. II. sempre col I.
Ihr tödtet Raupen in den Rosenknospen!
Ihr andern führt mit Fledermäusen Krieg,
Bringt ihrer Flügel Balg als Beute heim,
Den kleinen Elfen Röcke draus zu machen!
Ihr endlich sollt den Kauz, der nächtlich kreischt,
Und über unsre schmucken Geister staunt,
Von uns verscheuchen!
Singt mich nun in Schlaf!
An eure Dienste dann, und lasst mich ruhn!
arco
pp
Some, to kill cankers in the musk-rose buds!
Some, war with rear mice for their leathern wings,
To make my small elves coats!
And some, keep back
The clamorous owl, that nightly hoots, and wonders
At our quaint spirits.
Sing me now asleep!
Then to your offices, and let me rest!

pp
p
divisi
leggiero
Bun - te Schlan - gen, zwei - ge - züngt! I - gel, Mol - che, fort von hier! dass ihr
You sotted snakes, with dou - ble tongue, thor - ny hedge - hogs, be not seen; newts, and
Vcl.

cresc.
f
p
6
arco
eu - ren Gift nicht bringt in der Kö - ni - gin Re - vier, dass ihr
blind-worms, do no wrong; come not near our fai - ry queen, newts and
Bassi

6
6
6
dim.
dim.
divisi
pizz.
pp
pizz.
pp
eu - ren Gift nicht bringt in der Kö - ni - gin Re - vier, in der Kö - ni - gin Re - vier! Fort von
blind-worms, do no wrong, come not near our fai - ry queen, come not near our fai - ry queen. Hence a -
Vcl.
pizz.

p
cresc.
p
cresc.
pp
pp
p
hier!
fort von
hier!
Bun - te
Schlangen, zwei - ge - züngt!
I - gel,
way!
hence a - way!
You spotted sna - kes with double tongue,
thor - ny
pizz.
Bassi

a 2.
pp
pp
dim.
Mol - che, fort von hier! fort von hier! fort von hier!
hedge-hogs be not seen, hence a - way! hence a - way!

pp
p
ppp
arco
dol.
Nach_ti_gall, mit Me_lo_dei sing' in un_ser Ei_a_po_pei, Ei_apo_pei;
Phi_lo_mel, with me_lo_dy, sing in our sweet la lulla_by, la lulla_by,
Nach_ti_gall, mit Me_lo_dei sing' in un_ser Ei_a_po_pei, Ei_apo_pei apo_pei
Phi_lo_mel, with me_lo_dy, sing in our sweet la lulla_by, la lulla_by lullaby,
Vcl.

p
pizz.
pizz.
arco
pp
p
dass kein Spruch, kein Zauber - fluch der hol-den Herrin schädlich sei. Nun gu-te Nacht,
ne-ver harm, nor spell nor charm, come our love-ly la - dy nigh. So, so good night,
— apopei-a-po-pei; dass kein Spruch, kein Zauber - fluch der hol-den Herrin schädlich sei. Nun gu-te Nacht,
— lulla-by, lulla - by, ne-ver harm, nor spell nor charm, come our love-ly la - dy nigh. So, so good night,
pp
— apopei-a-po-pei; dass kein Spruch der Herrin schädlich sei. Nun gu-te Nacht,
— lulla-by, lulla - by, ne - ver harm, our love-ly la - dy nigh. So, so good night,
— apopei-a-po-pei; dass kein Spruch der Herrin schädlich sei. Nun gu-te Nacht,
— lulla-by, lulla - by, ne - ver harm, our love-ly la - dy nigh. So, so good night,
— apopei-a-po-pei; dass kein Spruch der Herrin schädlich sei. Nun gu-te
— lulla-by, lulla - by, ne - ver harm, our love-ly la - dy nigh. So, so good
— apopei-a-po-pei; dass kein Spruch der Herrin schädlich sei. Nun
— lulla-by, lulla - by, ne - ver harm, our love-ly la - dy nigh. So,
pizz.
Vcl.
arco
Bassi

pp
arco
pizz.
ppp
nun gu - te Nacht, gu_te Nacht mit Ei_a_po_pei. Nun gu_te Nacht,
so, so good night, so good night with la lulla - by! So, so good night,
nun gu - te Nacht mit Ei_a_po_pei. Nun
so, so good night with la lulla - by! So,
nun gu - te Nacht mit Ei_a_po_pei. Nun gu_te Nacht,
so, so good night with la lulla - by! So, so good night,
nun gu - te Nacht mit Ei_a_po_pei. Nun gute
so, so good night with la lulla - by! So, so good
Nacht, nun gu - te Nacht mit Ei_a_po_pei. Nun
night, so, so good night with la lulla - by! So,
gute Nacht, nun gu_te Nacht mit Ei_a_po_pei. Nun
so good night, good night, good night with la lulla - by! So,
sf
Vcl. arco
Bassi

arco
cresc.
pizz.
gu_te Nacht, nun gu_te Nacht, gu_te Nacht mit Ei_a_po_pei. Gu_te Nacht, gu_te
so good night, so, so good night, so good night with la lulla_by. So good night, so good
gute Nacht, nun gu_te Nacht mit Ei_a_po_pei. Gu_te Nacht
so good night, so, so good night with la lulla_by. So good night
nun gu_te Nacht mit Ei_a_po_pei. Gu_te Nacht,
so, so good night with la lulla_by. So good night,
Nacht, nun gu_te Nacht mit Ei_a_po_pei. Gu_te Nacht,
night, so, so good night with la lulla_by. So good night,
gu_te Nacht, nun gu_te Nacht mit Ei_a_po_pei. Gu_te Nacht,
so good night, so, so good night with la lulla_by. So good night,
gute Nacht, nun gu_te Nacht mit Ei_a_po_pei. Gu_te Nacht,
so good night, good night, good night with la lulla_by. So good night,
Bassi

pp

dim.

pp

dim.

dim.

dim.

pizz. arco

pizz.

pizz.

Nacht mit Ei_a_po_pei, gu_te Nacht, nun gu_te Nacht mit Ei_a_po_pei, a_po_pei!
night with la lulla_by, so good night, good night, good night with la lulla_by, lul_la_by!

mit Ei_a_po_pei, gu_te Nacht mit Ei_a_po_pei, nun gu_te Nacht mit Ei_a_po_pei!
with la lulla_by, so good night with la lulla_by, good night, good night with la lul_la_by!

pp

gu_te Nacht, nun gu_te Nacht mit Ei_a_po_pei!

pp

so good night, good night, good night with la lul_la_by!

pp

gu_te Nacht, nun gu_te Nacht mit Ei_a_po_pei!

pp

so good night, good night, good night with la lul_la_by!

pizz.

pp
pp
pp
p
arco
Schwarze
Wea_ving
arco
cresc.

pp
pp
pizz.
pizz.
divisi
pp
Kä - fer, uns um - gebt nicht mit Sum_men, macht euch fort! Spin_nen, die ihr künstlich webt, webt an
spi - ders, come not here: hence, you long-legg'd spin_ners, hence: beet - les black, approach not near, worm, nor
pizz.

cresc.
cresc.
p
p
cresc.
pp
cresc.
divisi
cresc.
pp
ei _ nem an_dern Ort, Spin_nen, die ihr künst_lich webt, webt an
snail, do no of - fence, beet _ les black, approach not near, worm, nor
arco
cresc.
pizz.

p cresc.
p cresc.
cresc.
p
cresc.
p
dimin.
cresc.
p
cresc.
Macht euch fort!
Hence a - way!
ei - nem an - dern Ort, webt an ei - nem an - dern Ort! Macht euch fort! Macht euch
snail, do no of - fence, worm, nor snail, do no of - fence. Hence a - way! Hence a -

Macht euch fort!
Hence a - way!
Macht euch
Hence a -
fort!
way!
Schwarze Kä - fer, uns um - gebt nicht mit Sum - men, macht euch fort!
Wea - ving spi - ders, come not here: hence, you long - legg'd spin - ners, hence:
arco
p
pp

a 2.
arco
dim.
pp
p
dol.
fort!
way!
Macht euch fort,
Hence a - way!
macht euch fort!
hence a - way!
Nach-ti-gall, mit
Phi-lo-mel, with
Macht euch fort,
Hence a - way!
macht euch fort!
hence a - way!
Nach-ti-gall, mit
Phi-lo-mel, with
Nach-ti-gall, mit
Phi-lo-mel, with
Nach-ti-gall, mit
Phi-lo-mel, with

Me - lo-dei sing' in un-ser Ei - a-popei, Ei-apo-pei; dass kein
me - lo-dy sing in our sweet la lulla-by, la lulla-by, ne-ver
Me - lo-dei sing' in un-ser Ei - a-popei, Ei-apo-pei apo-pei apopei-apo-pei; dass kein
me - lo-dy sing in our sweet la lulla-by, la lulla-by lulla-by lulla-by lulla - by, ne-ver
Me - lo-dei sing' in un-ser Ei - a-popei, Ei-apo-pei apo-pei apopei-apo-pei;
me - lo-dy sing in our sweet la lulla-by, la lulla-by lulla-by lulla-by lulla - by,
Me - lo-dei sing' in un-ser Ei - a-popei, Ei-apo-pei apo-pei apopei-apo-pei;
me - lo-dy sing in our sweet la lulla-by, la lulla-by lulla-by lulla-by lulla - by,

trem.

trem.

arco

Spruch, kein Zauber_fluch der holden Herrin schädlich sei. Nun gu_te Nacht, nun gu_te
harm, nor spell nor charm, come our lovely la_dy nigh. So, so good night, so, so good

Spruch, kein Zauber_fluch der holden Herrin schädlich sei. Nun gu_te Nacht, nun gu_te
harm, nor spell nor charm, come our lovely la_dy nigh. So, so good night, so, so good

dass kein Spruch der Herrin schädlich sei. Nun gu_te Nacht, nun gu_te
ne_ver harm, our lovely la_dy nigh. So, so good night, so, so good

dass kein Spruch der Herrin schädlich sei. Nun gu_te Nacht, nun gu_te
ne_ver harm, our lovely la_dy nigh. So, so good night, so, so good

dass kein Spruch der Herrin schädlich sei. Nun gu_te Nacht, nun gu_te
ne_ver harm, our lovely la_dy nigh. So, so good night, so, so good

dass kein Spruch der Herrin schädlich sei. Nun gu_te Nacht, nun
ne_ver harm, our lovely la_dy nigh. So, so good night, good

pizz. Vcl. arco arco

Bassi

cresc.
cresc.
cresc.
pizz.
pizz.
pizz.
arco
trem.
cresc.
arco
trem.
cresc.
arco
pp
cresc.
Nacht, gute Nacht mit Ei_apo_pei. Nun gute Nacht, gute Nacht, nun gu_te
night, so good night with la lulla_by! So, so good night, so good night, so, so good
Nacht mit Ei_apo_pei. Nun gute Nacht, nun gu_te
night with la lulla_by! So, so good night, so, so good
Nacht mit Ei_apo_pei. Nun gute Nacht, nun gu_te
night with la lulla_by! So, so good night, so, so good
Nacht mit Ei_apo_pei. Nun gute Nacht, nun gu_te
night with la lulla_by! So, so good night, so, so good
Nacht mit Ei_apo_pei. Nun gute Nacht,
night with la lulla_by! So, so good night,
gu_te Nacht mit Ei_apo_pei. Nun gute Nacht,
night, good night with la lulla_by! So, so good night,
pizz.
arco
cresc.

tr
p
pp
pizz.
arco
Nacht, gute Nacht mit Ei_apo_pei. Gu_te Nacht, gu_te Nacht mit Ei_a_po_pei, gu_te Nacht, nun gu_te
night, so good night with la lulla_by. So good night, so good night with la lulla_by, so good night, good night, good
Nacht mit Ei_apo_pei. Gu_te Nacht mit Ei_a_po_pei, gu_te Nacht
night with la lulla_by. So good night with la lulla_by, so good night
Nacht mit Ei_apo_pei. Gu_te Nacht, gu_te Nacht,
night with la lulla_by. So good night, so good night,
nun gute Nacht mit Ei_apo_pei. Gu_te Nacht, gu_te Nacht,
so, so good night with la lulla_by. So good night, so good night,

pp
pp
pp
pp
pizz.
Nacht mit Ei_a_po_pei a_po_pei! Al_les gut!
night with la lulla_by lul_la_by! Hence, a_way!
mit Ei_a_po_pei, nun gu_te Nacht mit Ei_a_po_pei!
with la lulla_by, good night, good night with la lul_la_by!
nun gu_te Nacht mit Ei_a_po_pei!
good night, good night with la lul_la_by!
nun gu_te Nacht mit Ei_a_po_pei!
good night, good night with la lul_la_by!
arco
cresc.
dim.

pp
arco
trem.
ten.
pizz.
Nun auf und fort! Ei - ner hal-te Wa - che dort!
now all is well: One, a-loof, stand sen - ti - nel.
Vcl.
Bassi
(Oberon tritt auf.)
(Enter Oberon.)
attacca

No. 4. Andante.
Flauti.
Clarinetti in A.
Fagotti.
Violino I.
Bassi.
Oberon.
Was du wirst erwachend seh'n —
Wähl' es dir zum Liebchen schön,
Seinetwegen schmacht' und stöhn'.
Sei es Brummbär, Kater, Luchs,
Borst'ger Eber oder Fuchs;
Was sich zeigt an diesem Platz,
con sordino
pp
What thou seest, when thou dost wake,
Do it for thy true love take;
Love, and languish for his sake!
Be it ounce, or cat, or bear,
Pard, or boar, with bristled hair,
In thy eye that shall appear
Andante.
Wenn du aufwachst, wird dein Schatz;
Siehst du gleich die ärgste Fratz!
Allegro molto.
When thou wak'st, it is thy dear;
Wake, when some vile thing is near.
Allegro molto.
(Oberon verschwindet.)
(Oberon exit.)
(Lysander u. Hermia kommen.)
Dialog bis:
Puck.
Die Arme darf nicht liegen näh
Dem Schlagetodt der Liebe da.
(Enter Lys. and Herm.)
Dialogue till:
Puck.
Pretty soul! she durst not lie
Near this lack-love, kill-courtesy.
Andante.
Puck.
Allen Zauber dieses Thau's, Flegel, giess' ich auf dich aus.
Wach'st du auf, so scheuch' den Schlummer dir vom Aug' der Liebe Kummer!
Churl, upon thy eyes I throw All the power this charm doth owe:
When thou wak'st, let love forbid Sleep his seat on thy eye-lid
Viola.
senza sordino
Andante.
Allegro molto.
Nun erwach', ich geh' davon, denn ich muss zum Oberon.
(Puck verschwindet.)
So awake, when I am gone; For I must now to Oberon.
(Puck exit.)
Allegro molto.
(Demetrius und Helena kommen.)
pizz.
(Enter Demetrius and Helena.)

Hermia. Dich muss ich, oder meinen Tod ereilen.
Hermia. *Either death, or you, I'll find immediately.*

Nº5. (Nach dem Schlusse des zweiten Aktes.) *(After the end of the second act.)*

Allegro appassionato.

cresc.
f
sf
p
dim.
pizz.
arco
a 2.
mf

sempre a 2.
cresc.
p cresc.
sempre a 2.
cresc.
p cresc.
cresc.
cresc.
pizz.
sf
sf
sf
f
f<>
dim.
p
p
dim.
dim.
dim.
arco
pizz.
sf

dim.
p
cresc.
sf
dim.
pp
f
arco
pizz.
mf

cresc.
dim.
sf
p
pp
a 2.
pizz.
arco
al

cresc.
cresc.
cresc.
cresc.
cresc.
f
p
cresc.
f
pizz.
a 2.
p cresc.
f
dim.
p
dim.
arco
p cresc. molto
pizz.
cresc.

sf
f
p
dim.
pizz.
pp

Allegro molto comodo.

Allegro molto comodo.

a 2.
p
cresc.
sf
sf
cresc.
p cresc.
pp
arco
pp
arco
pp
arco
pp

Zettel. Sind wir alle beisammen?
Bottom. *Are we all met?*

Squenz. Wann ihr eure Rede ausgeredet habt, so tretet hinter den Busch; und so jeder nach seinem Stichwort.
No 6. Allegro.
Flauti.
Oboi.
Clarinetti in A.
Fagotti.
Ophicleïde.
Violino I.
Violino II.
Viola.
Violoncello e Basso.
Quince. When you have spoken your speech, enter into that brake; and so every one according to his cue.
Puck (kommt.)
Welch' hausgebacknes Volk macht sich hier breit,
So nah der Wiege unsrer Königin?
Wie? gibt's ein Schauspiel?
Ich will Hörer sein,
Mitspieler auch vielleicht, nach dem
Enter Puck.
What hempen home-spuns have we swaggering here,
So near the cradle of the fairy queen?
What, a play toward?
I'll be an auditor;
An actor too, perhaps, if I see cause.
divisi
pizz.
arco
Allegro.
sich's fügt.
(Squenz spricht) bis:
Pyramus.
Bleib' eine Weile stehn, ich bin gleich wieder hier.
Puck.
Ein seltnes Stück von einem Pyramus.
Squenz.
Pyramus, tretet auf; euer Stichwort ist schon dagewesen; es ist: ermüdet auch.
Dialog bis:
Thisbe.
Uf_ So treu, wie's treuste Pferd, das nie ermüdet auch.
Thisbe.
O,_ As true as truest horse, that yet would never tire.
(Quince speaks till:)
Dialogue till:
Pyramus.
And by, and by I will tho thee appear.
Puck.
A stranger Pyramus than e'er play'd here!
Quince.
Pyramus enter; your cue is past; it is: never tire.

ritard.

ritard.

Hund und Bär,

Erschein' als Wehrwolf und als Feuer bald,

Will grunzen, wiehern,

bellen, brummen, flammen,

Wie Eber, Pferd, Hund, Bär und Feu'r zusammen.

Zettel (allein.)

Warum laufen sie weg? dies ist eine Schelmerei von ihnen, um mich fürchten zu machen.

ritard.

(Puck ab.)

Bottom (alone.)

Why do they run away? this is a knavery of them, to make me afeard.

sometime a hound, A hog, a headless bear, sometime a fire; And neigh, and bark, and grunt, and roar, and burn, Like horse, hound, hog, bear, fire, at every turn.

(Exit.)

Schnauz (kommt zurück.)
O Zettel, du bist verwandelt! Was seh' ich an dir?

Zettel.
Was du siehst? Du siehst deinen eignen Eselskopf! Nicht?

(*Dialog* geht fort) bis:

Zettel (singt nach beliebiger Melodie.)
Die Lerche, die sich lustig schwingt Bis in den Himmel 'nein.

Titania (erwacht und spricht:)
Weckt mich von meinem Blumenbett' ein Engel?

Zettel (singt und spricht:) bis:
Wem juckt es nicht ein bischen an der Stirne, wenn er sich Kukuk grüssen hört?

pp I. **Titania.**
Ich bitte dich, du holder Sterblicher,
Sing' noch einmal! Mein Ohr ist ganz verliebt
In deine Melodie.

Dialogue continues till:

Corni in E.
II. pp

(*Re-enter* Snout.)
O Bottom, thou ar changed! what do I see on the?

Bottom.
What do you see? you see an ass' head of your own: Do you?

Bottom (*sings to his own tune.*)
The throstle with his note so true, The wren with little quill.

Titania (*waking.*)
What angel wakes me from my flowery bed?

Bottom (*sings and speaks till:*)
Who would give a bird the lie, though he cry cuckoo, never so?

Titania (*speaks:*)
*I pray thee, gentle mortal, sing again:
Mine ear is much enamourl'd of thy note.*

Tempo Allegro.

Titania.
Auch ist mein Aug' bethört pp.

(*Dialog* geht fort) bis:

Senfsamen!
Bohnenblüthe!
Motte!
Spinnweb!

Fl.
Ob.
Clr.
Fag.
(Vier Elfen treten auf.)
Cor.

I^ter Elfe. Hier!
II^ter Elfe. Und ich!
III^ter Elfe. Und ich!
IV^ter Elfe. Wohin heisst du uns gehen?
Alle. Was sollen wir?
Titania. Gefällig seid und dienstbar pp bis:
Nun, Elfen, huldigt ihm, und neigt euch fein.

(Die Elfen verneigen sich.)

Viol. I.
(*Enter four Fairies.*)
Viol. II.
Viola.
Bassi.

Corni.
Viola.
pp

Titania *continues to speak:*
So is mine eye enthralled etc. till:
Peas blossom! Cobweb! Moth! and Mustard-seed!

1. Fairy. *Ready.*
2. Fairy. *And I.*
3. Fairy. *And I.*
4. Fairy. *Where shall we go?*

Titania.
Be kind and courteous etc. till:
Nod to him, elves, and do him courtesies.

(*The elves bow.*)

Tempo Allegro.

p pp

Zettel.

Ich flehe Euer Gnaden um Vergebung. pp.

Dialog bis:

Ich wünsche nähere Bekanntschaft, lieber Musje Senfsamen.

pp pp

I^ter^ Elfe. Heil dir, Sterblicher!

II^ter^ Elfe. Heil!

III^ter^ Elfe. Heil!

IV^ter^ Elfe. Heil!

Titania.

Kommt, führt ihn hin zu meinem Heiligthume!

Mich dünkt, von Thränen blinke Luna's Glanz;

Und wenn sie weint, weint jede kleine Blume

1. Fairy. *Hail, mortal!*

2. Fairy. *Hail!*

3. Fairy. *Hail!*

4. Fairy. *Hail!*

Bottom.

I cry your worships mercy, etc.

Dialogue till:

I desire you more acquaintance, good master Mustard-seed.

Titania.

Come, wait upon him; lead him to my bower.

The moon, methinks, looks with a watry eye;

And when she weeps, weeps every little flower,

Oberon (kommt.)

Mich wundert's, ob Titania erwachte,

Und welch' Geschöpf ihr gleich in's Auge fiel,

Worin sie sterblich sich verlieben muss.

(Puck kommt.)

Da kommt mein Bote ja. Nun, toller Geist,

p pp

Um einen wild zerrissnen Mädchenkranz.

Ein Zauber soll des Liebsten Zunge binden:

Wir wollen still den Weg zur Laube finden. (Alle ab.)

Enter **Oberon.**

I wonder, if Titania be awak'd;

Then, what it was that next came in her eye,

Which she must dote on in extremity.

(Enter Puck.)

Lamenting some enforced chastity.

Tie up my love's tongue, bring him silently.

(Exeunt.)

Here comes my messenger.— How now, mad spirit?

pizz. p

Allegro molto.

Fl. I. *f* *dim.*

Ob. I. *f* *dim.*

Cl. *p*

Fag. *p*

Viol. *p* *cresc.*

Viola.

Bassi.

Was spuken hier im Wald für Abenteuer?

What night-rule now about this haunted grove?

Puck.
Herr, meine Fürstin liebt ein Ungeheuer! pp.

Puck.
My mistress with a monster is in love, etc.

Dialog.

(Demetrius u. Hermia kommen.)

Dialog.

(Hermia ab. Demetrius schläft ein.)

Oberon.
Was thatest du? pp. bis:
Geh', locke sie durch Täuschung her zu mir;
Derweil sie kommt, bezaubr' ich diesen hier.

(Enter Demetrius and Helena.)

Dialogue.

(Hermia exit. Demetrius lies down.)

Oberon. *What hast thou done? till:*
By some illusion see thou bring her here;
I'll charm his eyes, against she do appear.

Allegro molto.

ritard. *pp*

pp *ritard.*

p

Puck.
Ich eil', ich eil', sieh' wie ich eil': so fliegt vom Bogen des Tartaren Pfeil!
(Puck ab.)

Puck.
I go, I go; look, how I go; Swifter than arrow from the Tartar's bow.
(Exit.)

Oberon.
Blume mit dem Purpurschein, Die Cupido's Pfeile weih'n, Senk' dich in sein Aug' hinein.

Oberon.
Flower of this purple dye, Hit with Cupid's archery, Sink in apple of his eye!

Tempo.
Wenn er sieht sein Liebchen fein,
Dass sie glorreich ihm erschein',
Wie Cyther' im Sternenreih'n.
Wachst du auf, wenn sie dabei,
Bitte, dass sie hülfreich sei.
(Puck kommt zurück.)
When his love he doth espy,
Let her shine as glori-ously
As the Venus of the sky.
When thou wak'st, if she be by,
Beg of her for remedy.
(Re-enter Puck.)
Tempo.

I.

f

dim.

I.

f

dim.

I. *p*

p

sf

cresc.

sf

sf

cresc.

sf

Puck.

Hauptmann unsrer Elfenschaar,

Hier stellt Helena sich dar.

Der von mir gesalbte Mann Fleht um Liebeslohn sie an. Wollen wir ihr Wesen seh'n?

Puck.

Captain of our fairy band,

Helena is here at hand,

And the youth, mistook by me, Pleading for a lover's fee; Shall we their fond pageant see?

I. *f* I. *f* *dim.* *dim.* I. *p* *p* *dim.* *dim.*

O die tollen Sterblichen!

Oberon.
Tritt beiseit'! Erwachen muss
Von dem Lärm Demetrius.

Puck.
Wenn dann zwei um eine frein: Das wird erst ein Hauptspass sein. Geh'n die Sachen kraus und bunt, freu' ich mich von Herzensgrund.

Lord, what fools these mortals be!

Oberon.
Stand aside: the noise they make,
Will cause Demetrius to awake.

Puck.
Then will two, at once, woo one, That must needs be sport alone; And those things do best please me, That befal preposterously.

Langer Dialog.

(Lysander und Helena treten auf.)
(Demetrius erwacht.)
(Hermia kommt.)
(Lysander und Demetrius ab.)
(Helena ab. Hermia läuft ihr nach.)
(Oberon und Puck bleiben allein) bis:

Oberon.
Doch zaudre nicht, sei schnell vor allen Dingen,
Wir können dies vor Tage noch vollbringen.

(Oberon ab.)

Dialogue.

(Enter Lysander and Helena.)
(Demetrius awakes.)
(Enter Hermia.)
(Exeunt Lysander and Demetrius.)
(Exit Hermia, pursuing Helena.)
(Oberon and Puck alone) till:

Oberon.
But, notwithstandig, haste; make no delay:
We may effect this business yet ere day.
(Exit Oberon.)

Andante.

pp *dim.* *pp*

Timpani in D.

pp *dim.*

Puck.
Hin und her, hin und her, Alle führ' ich hin und her, Land und Städte scheu'n mich sehr. Kobold, führ' sie hin und her! Da kommt der Eine.

Up and down, up and down; I will lead them up and down: I am fear'd in field and town; Goblin, lead them up and down. Here comes one.

Bassi

pp *dim.* *pp* *pp*

Andante.

Allegro molto come I.
pizz.
(Lysander kommt.)
Lysander: Demetrius! Wo bist du, Stolzer, Du?
pp
cresc.
dim.
I.
Lysander.
Where art thoy, proud Demetrius? speak thou now.
(Enter Lysander.)
Allegro molto come I.
Lysander.
Ich komme schon.
(Demetrius kommt.)
Demetrius.
Antworte doch, Lysander!
Puck.
Hier, Schurk', mit blossem Degen;
mach' nur zu!
Puck.
So lass uns mit einander auf ebnen Boden geh'n.
(Beide ab.)
Puck.
Here, villain, drawn and ready!
Where art thou?
Lysander.
I will be with thee straight.
sf cresc.
Puck.
Follow me then To plainer ground.
(Enter Demetrius.)
Demetrius.
Lysander, speak again!
(Exit Lysander following the voice.)

I. f
dim.
I. f
dim.
dim.
pizz.
Puck.
Ausreisser! Memme! Liefst du so mir fort?
Du Memme, forderst hier heraus die Sterne,
Erzählst dem Busch, du föchtest gar zu gerne, Und kommst doch nicht?
Komm, Bübchen, komm doch her! Ich geb' die Ruthe dir.
Beschimpft ist der, der gegen dich nur zieht.
Demetrius.
He, bist du dort?
Puck.
Folg' meinem Ruf, zum Kampf ist dies kein Ort.
In welchem Busche steckst du? sprich ein Wort!
Thou runaway, thou coward, art thou fled?
Thou coward, art thou bragging to the stars,
Telling the bushes that thou look'st for wars, And wilt not come?
Come, recreant; come, thou child; I'll whip thee with a rod:
He is defil'd, that draws a sword on thee.
Speak! In some bush? Where dost thou hide thy head?
Demetrius.
Yea; art thou there?
Puck.
Follow my voice; we'll try no manhood here.
pizz.
(Beide ab.)
(Lysander kommt zurück.)
Lysander.
Stets zieht er vor mir her
mit lautem Droh'n,
komm' ich, wohin er ruft, ist er entfloh'n.
arco
Lysander.
He goes before me, and still dares me on;
When I come where he calls, then he is gone.
(Exeunt.)
(Re-enter Lysander.)

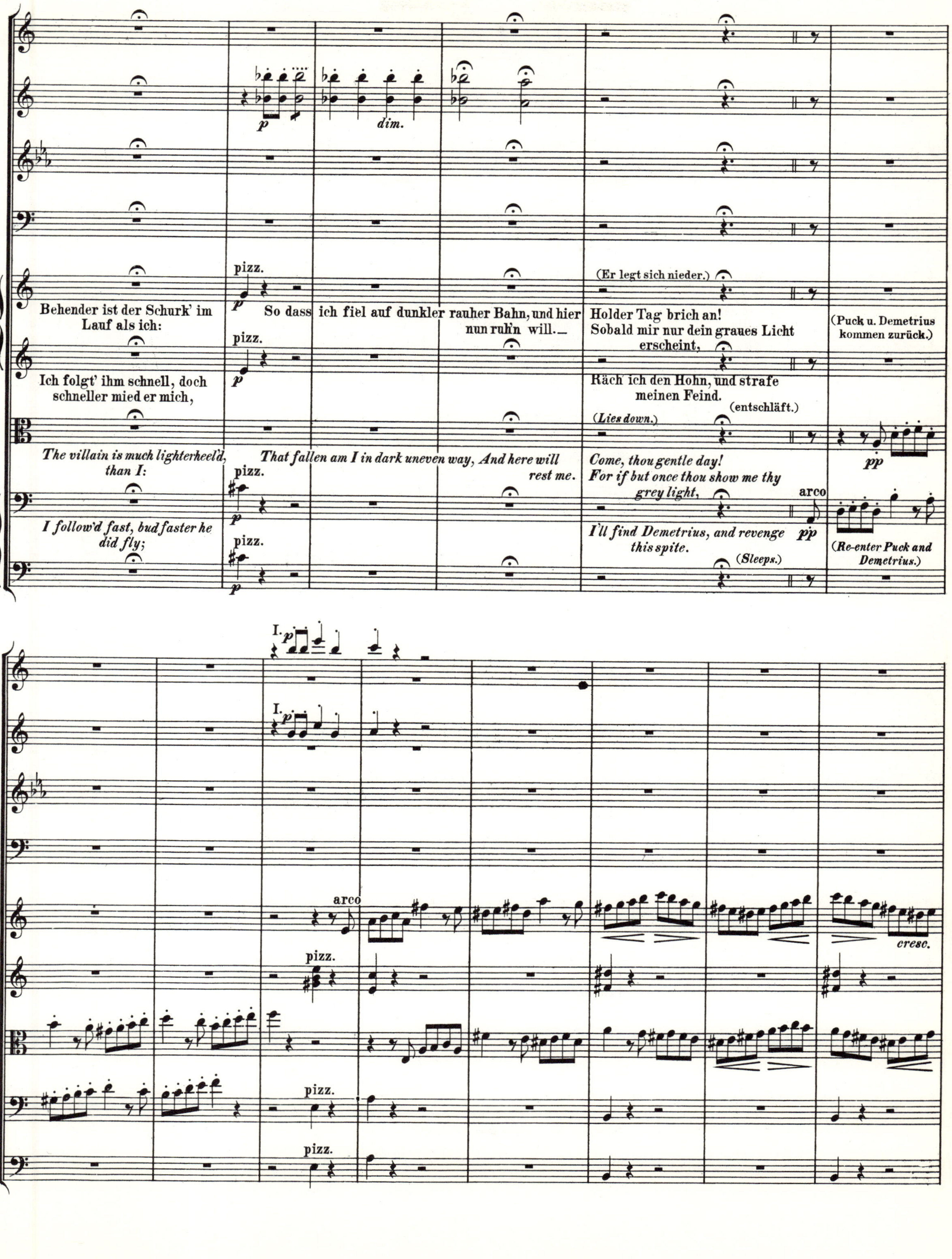

pizz. p dim.

Behender ist der Schurk' im Lauf als ich: So dass ich fiel auf dunkler rauher Bahn, und hier nun ruh'n will.—

(Er legt sich nieder.) Holder Tag brich an! Sobald mir nur dein graues Licht erscheint,

Ich folgt' ihm schnell, doch schneller mied er mich,

Räch ich den Hohn, und strafe meinen Feind. (entschläft.)

(Puck u. Demetrius kommen zurück.)

(Lies down.)

The villain is much lighterheel'd, than I: That fallen am I in dark uneven way, And here will rest me.

Come, thou gentle day! For if but once thou show me thy grey light,

I follow'd fast, bud faster he did fly;

I'll find Demetrius, and revenge this spite. *(Sleeps.)*

arco pp

(Re-enter Puck and Demetrius.)

I. p I. p arco pizz. pizz. pizz. cresc.

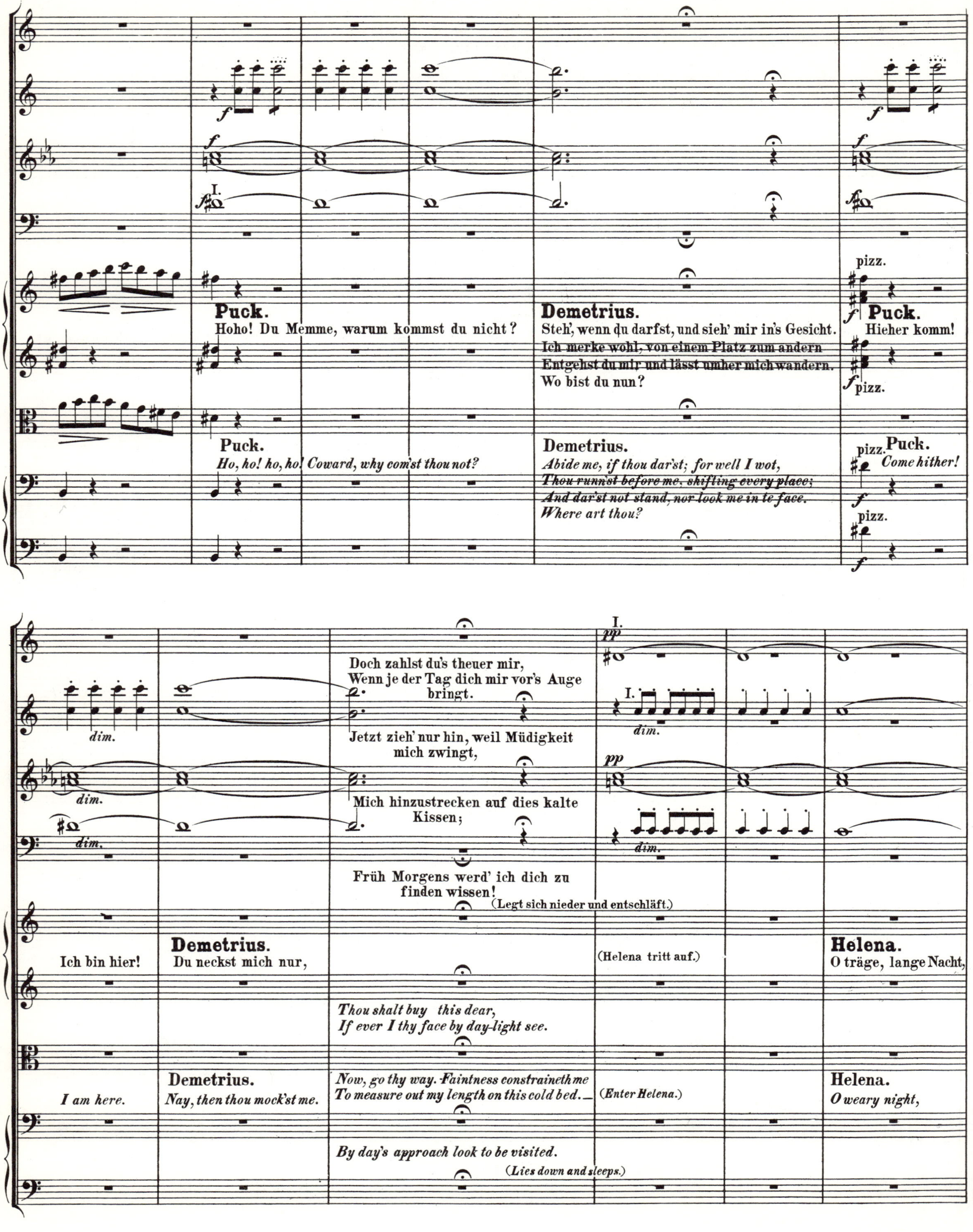

I.

pizz.

Puck.
Hoho! Du Memme, warum kommst du nicht?

Ho, ho! ho, ho! Coward, why com'st thou not?

Demetrius.
Steh', wenn du darfst, und sieh' mir in's Gesicht.
Ich merke wohl, von einem Platz zum andern
Entgehst du mir und lässt umher mich wandern.
Wo bist du nun?

Abide me, if thou dar'st; for well I wot,
Thou runn'st before me, shifting every place;
And dar'st not stand, nor look me in te face.
Where art thou?

Puck.
Hieher komm!

Come hither!

Ich bin hier!

I am here.

Demetrius.
Du neckst mich nur,

Nay, then thou mock'st me.

Doch zahlst du's theuer mir,
Wenn je der Tag dich mir vor's Auge bringt.
Jetzt zieh' nur hin, weil Müdigkeit mich zwingt,
Mich hinzustrecken auf dies kalte Kissen;
Früh Morgens werd' ich dich zu finden wissen!
(Legt sich nieder und entschläft.)

Thou shalt buy this dear,
If ever I thy face by day-light see.
Now, go thy way. Faintness constraineth me
To measure out my length on this cold bed.—
By day's approach look to be visited.
(Lies down and sleeps.)

(Helena tritt auf.)

(Enter Helena.)

Helena.
O träge, lange Nacht,

O weary night,

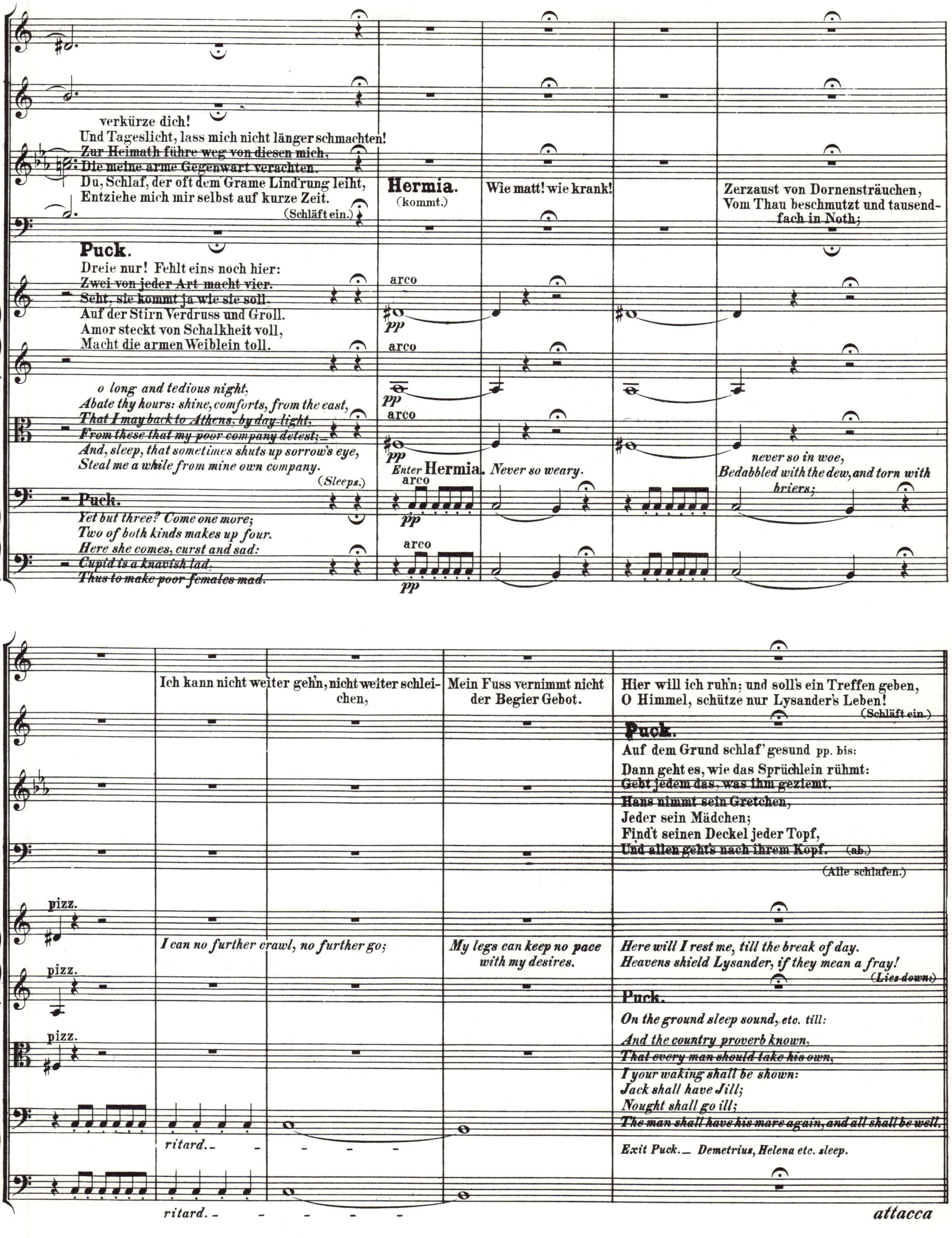

verkürze dich!
Und Tageslicht, lass mich nicht länger schmachten!
Zur Heimath führe weg von diesen mich,
Die meine arme Gegenwart verachten.
Du, Schlaf, der oft dem Grame Lind'rung leiht,
Entziehe mich mir selbst auf kurze Zeit.
(Schläft ein.)

Hermia. (kommt.)

Wie matt! wie krank!

Zerzaust von Dornensträuchen,
Vom Thau beschmutzt und tausendfach in Noth;

Puck.
Dreie nur! Fehlt eins noch hier:
Zwei von jeder Art macht vier.
Seht, sie kommt ja wie sie soll.
Auf der Stirn Verdruss und Groll.
Amor steckt von Schalkheit voll,
Macht die armen Weiblein toll.

arco *pp*

o long and tedious night,
Abate thy hours: shine, comforts, from the east,
That I may back to Athens, by day-light,
From these that my poor company detest;—
And, sleep, that sometimes shuts up sorrow's eye,
Steal me a while from mine own company.
(Sleeps.)

Enter **Hermia.** *Never so weary.*

never so in woe,
Bedabbled with the dew, and torn with briers;

Puck.
Yet but three? Come one more;
Two of both kinds makes up four.
Here she comes, curst and sad:
Cupid is a knavish lad,
Thus to make poor females mad.

Ich kann nicht weiter geh'n, nicht weiter schleichen,

Mein Fuss vernimmt nicht der Begier Gebot.

Hier will ich ruh'n; und soll's ein Treffen geben,
O Himmel, schütze nur Lysander's Leben!
(Schläft ein.)

Puck.
Auf dem Grund schlaf' gesund pp. bis:
Dann geht es, wie das Sprüchlein rühmt:
Gebt jedem das, was ihm geziemt.
Hans nimmt sein Gretchen,
Jeder sein Mädchen;
Find't seinen Deckel jeder Topf,
Und allen geht's nach ihrem Kopf. (ab.)
(Alle schlafen.)

pizz.

I can no further crawl, no further go;

My legs can keep no pace with my desires.

Here will I rest me, till the break of day.
Heavens shield Lysander, if they mean a fray!
(Lies down.)

Puck.
On the ground sleep sound, etc. till:
And the country proverb known,
That every man should take his own,
I your waking shall be shown:
Jack shall have Jill;
Nought shall go ill;
The man shall have his mare again, and all shall be well.

Exit Puck.— Demetrius, Helena etc. sleep.

ritard.

attacca

Nº 7. Con moto tranquillo.
Flauti.
Oboi.
Clarinetti in A.
Fagotti.
Corno I in E.
Corno II in E.
Violino I.
Violino II.
Viola.
Violoncello e Basso.
Con moto tranquillo.
p dol.
pp
cresc.
dim.
mf
f

cresc.
cresc.
cresc.
cresc.
cresc.
p
p
p
pp
pp
cresc. ed agitato
p
cresc.
p
cresc.
p
cresc.
cresc.
a 2.
mf
cresc.
sf
pp
pp
sf
pp
f
pp
f
pp
mf
pizz.
pp
f
arco

cresc.
pizz.
arco
Vcl.
Basso
pizz.

p *dim.* *p* *dim.* *p* *dim.* *p* *dim.* arco *dim.*

pp *p* *dol.* *pp* *pp* *pp* *pp* Bassi arco *pp*

pp
pp
cresc.
cresc.
cresc.
cresc.
cresc.
cresc.
cresc.
dim.
sf
dim.
dol.
f
dol.
dim.
pp
al
sf

pp
cresc.
f
dim.
p
pizz.
arco
(Hier öffnet sich die Laube wieder und man
sieht Titania und Zettel mit den Elfen.)
(Oberon im Hintergrunde verborgen.)
(The bower opens again; it is to see
Titania and Bottom with the elves.)
(Oberon behind, unseen.)
tr

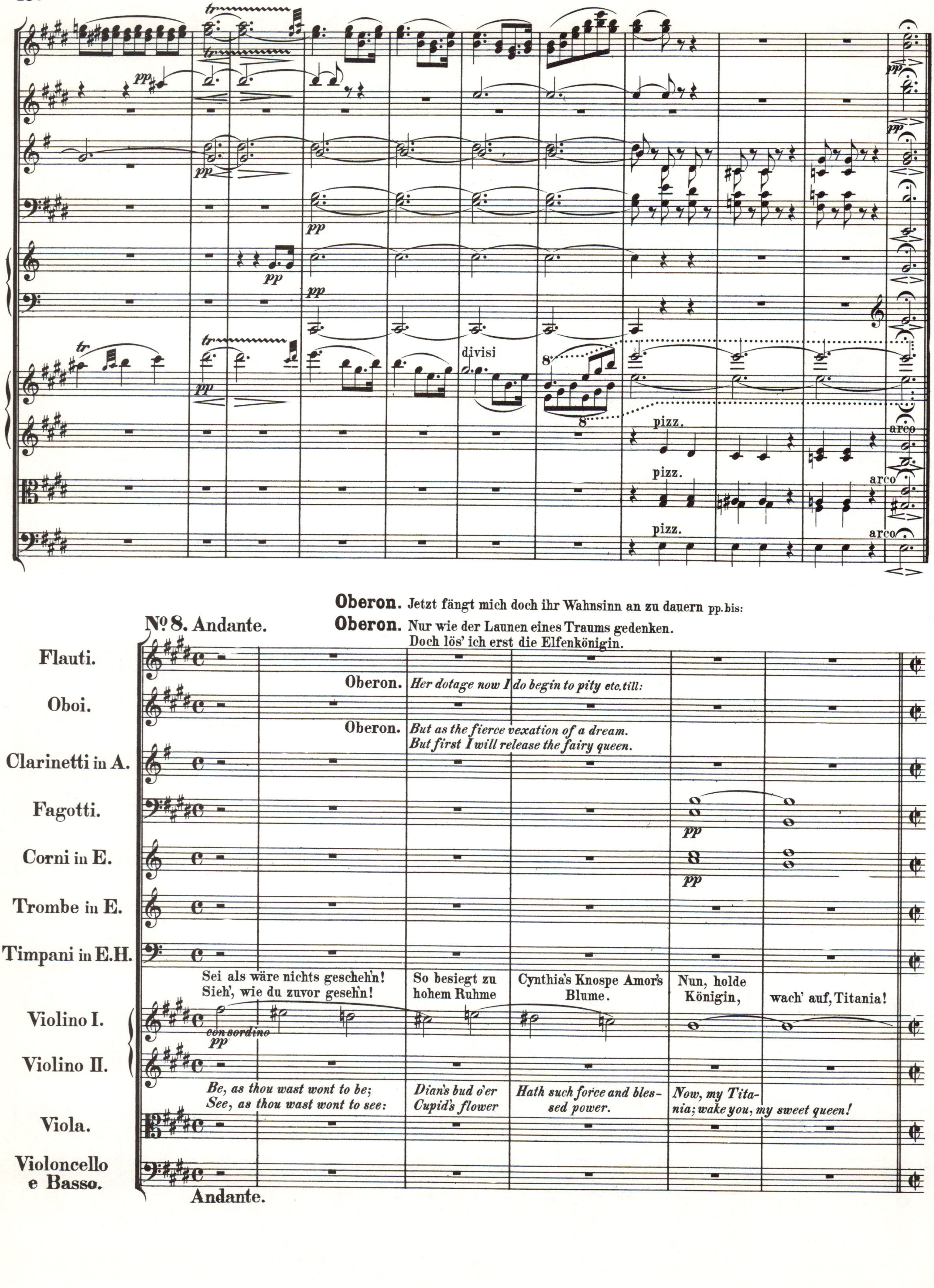

Oberon. Jetzt fängt mich doch ihr Wahnsinn an zu dauern pp. bis:

Oberon. Nur wie der Launen eines Traums gedenken.
Doch lös' ich erst die Elfenkönigin.

Oberon. *Her dotage now I do begin to pity etc. till:*

Oberon. *But as the fierce vexation of a dream.*
But first I will release the fairy queen.

Nº 8. Andante.

Flauti.

Oboi.

Clarinetti in A.

Fagotti.

Corni in E.

Trombe in E.

Timpani in E.H.

Violino I.

Violino II.

Viola.

Violoncello e Basso.

Sei als wäre nichts gescheh'n! Sieh', wie du zuvor geseh'n! So besiegt zu hohem Ruhme Cynthia's Knospe Amor's Blume. Nun, holde Königin, wach' auf, Titania!

Be, as thou wast wont to be; See, as thou wast wont to see: Dian's bud o'er Cupid's flower Hath such force and blessed power. Now, my Titania; wake you, my sweet queen!

con sordino

Andante.

Con moto tranquillo.
Allegro molto.
pp
(Titania erwacht.)
(Titania awakes.)
Dialog bis:
Puck.
Wenn du erwachst, so sollst du umgeschaffen,
Aus deinen eignen, dummen Augen gaffen.
Oberon.
Ertön' Musik.
Dialogue till:
Puck.
Now, when thou wak'st, with thine own fool's eyes peep.
Oberon.
Sound, music!
Oberon. Nun
senza
Oberon. Come,
Allegro molto.
Con moto tranquillo.
NB. Die Flöte hält aus bis zum Stichwort.
NB. The Flute holds the tune till the cue.
(Dialog geht fort) bis:
komm, Gemalin, Hand in Hand gefügt,
Und dieser Schläfer
Ruheplatz gewiegt!
Die Freundschaft zwischen uns ist nun erneut.
Auch werden da vermält zu gleicher Zeit
Die Paare hier in Wonn' und Fröhlichkeit.
sordino
(Dialogue continues) till:
my queen, take hands with me,
And rock the ground whereon these slepers be.
Now thou and I are new in amity;
There shall the pairs of faithful lovers be
Wedded, with Theseus, all in jollity.

pp

pp

pp

pp

arco

pizz.

a 2.

pizz.

pizz.

(Sie verschwinden.)

(Kurze Fermate u. gleich weiter.)

(Theseus, Hyppolita, Egeus und Gefolge treten auf.)

(Exeunt.)

(Short pause.)

(Enter Theseus, Hippolyta, Egeus and Train.)

Ophicleïde.

Timpani in E.

Violino I. II.

Dialog.

Theseus.

Sie machten ohne Zweifel früh sich auf pp. bis:

Geh', heiss' die Jäger sie mit ihren Hörnern wecken.

Dialogue.

Theseus.

No doubt, they rose up early, to observe etc. till:

Go, bid the huntsmen wake them with their horns.

(Sie erwachen und fahren auf.)

(They awake and start up.)

Nº 9. HOCHZEITMARSCH. (Nach dem Schlusse des vierten Aktes.)
WEDDING MARCH. (after the end of the fourth act.)

1.
tr
a 3.
f
2 u. 3 unis.
1.

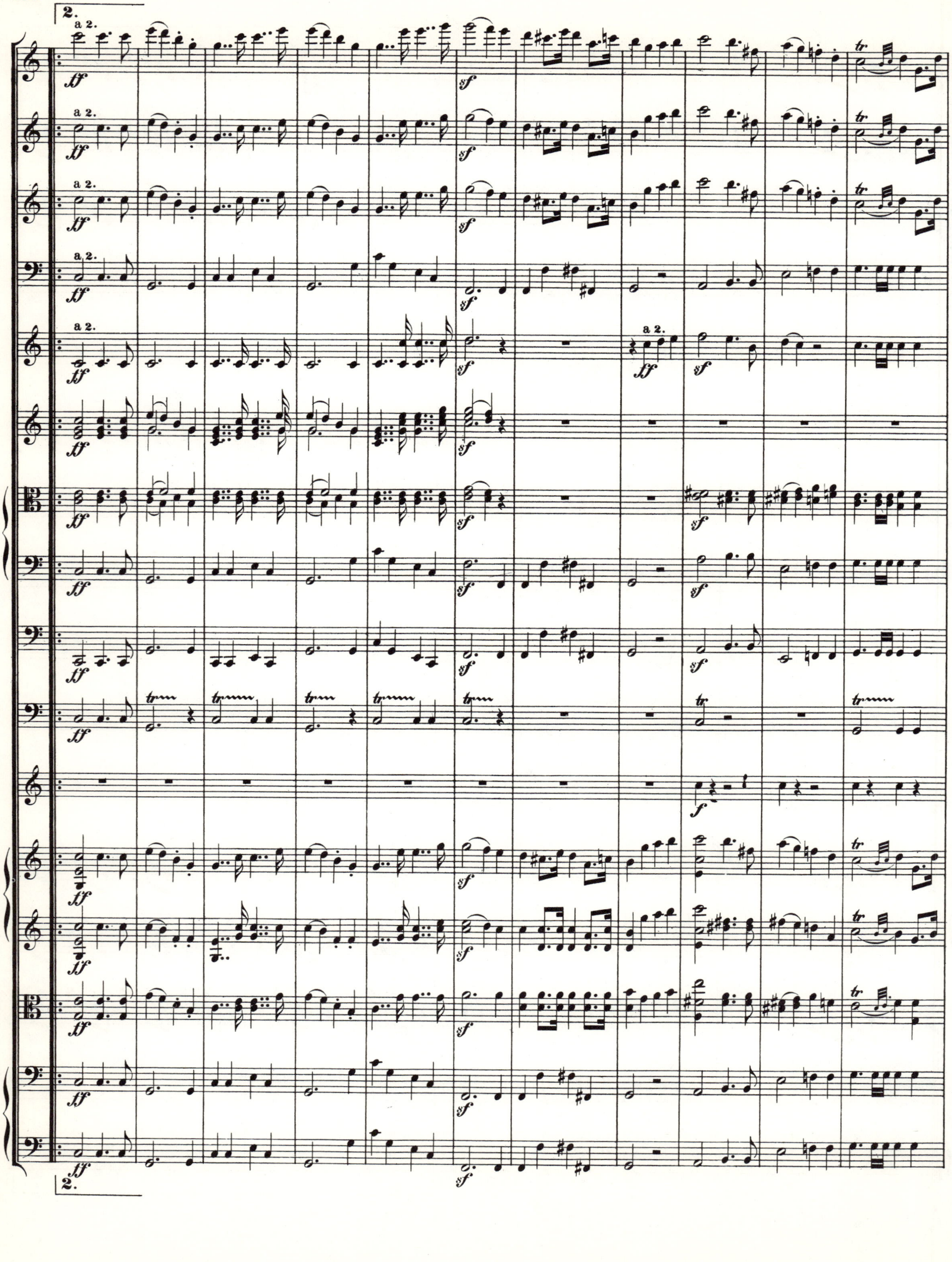
2.
a 2.
ff
sf
tr
f

1.
2.
tr
f
sf
a 2.
a 3.
trm

1.
2.
a 2.
a 3.
1.
2.

1.
2.
a 2.
sf
f
ff
a 3.
tr
1.
2.

tr
a 2.
p
sf
pizz.

p
p
sf
sf
p
sf
p
sf
p
a 2.
p
sf
p
cresc.
sf
p
cresc.
sf
p
cresc.
sf
p
cresc.
arco
sf
cresc.

a 2.
p
cresc.
sf
molto cresc.
a 3.
f

Der Vorhang auf. (Der Hochzeitzug kommt.)
The curtain is drawn. (Enter the wedding procession.)

a 2.
a 2
a 3.
tr
sf
ff
ff sf
f

a 2.
tr
a 2.
a 2.
tr
a 2.
tr
a 2.
a 3.
tr
tr

Hyppolita. Was diese Liebenden erzählen pp.

Hyppolita. *'Tis strange, my Theseus, that these lovers speak of etc.*

Philostrat. Beliebt es eurer Hoheit? Der Prolog ist fertig.

Theseus. Aber kommt, Euren Tanz; den Epilog lasst laufen.
Theseus. *But come, your Bergomask; let your epilogue alone.*

Nº 11. EIN TANZ VON RÜPELN. — A DANCE OF CLOWNS.

a 2.
Bassi
a 2.
a 2.
a 2.
a 2.

a 2.
dim.
p
ff
Theseus (unterbricht den Tanz mit den Worten:)
Die Mitternacht rief zwölf pp. bis:
Zu Bett, geliebten Freunde!
Noch vierzehn Tage lang soll diese Festlichkeit
Sich jede Nacht erneu'n, mit Spiel und Lustbarkeit.
Theseus (breaks up the dance:)
The iron tongue of midnight hath told twelve, till:
Sweet friends, to bed.—
A fortnight hold we this solemnity,
In nightly revels, and new jollity.
attacca

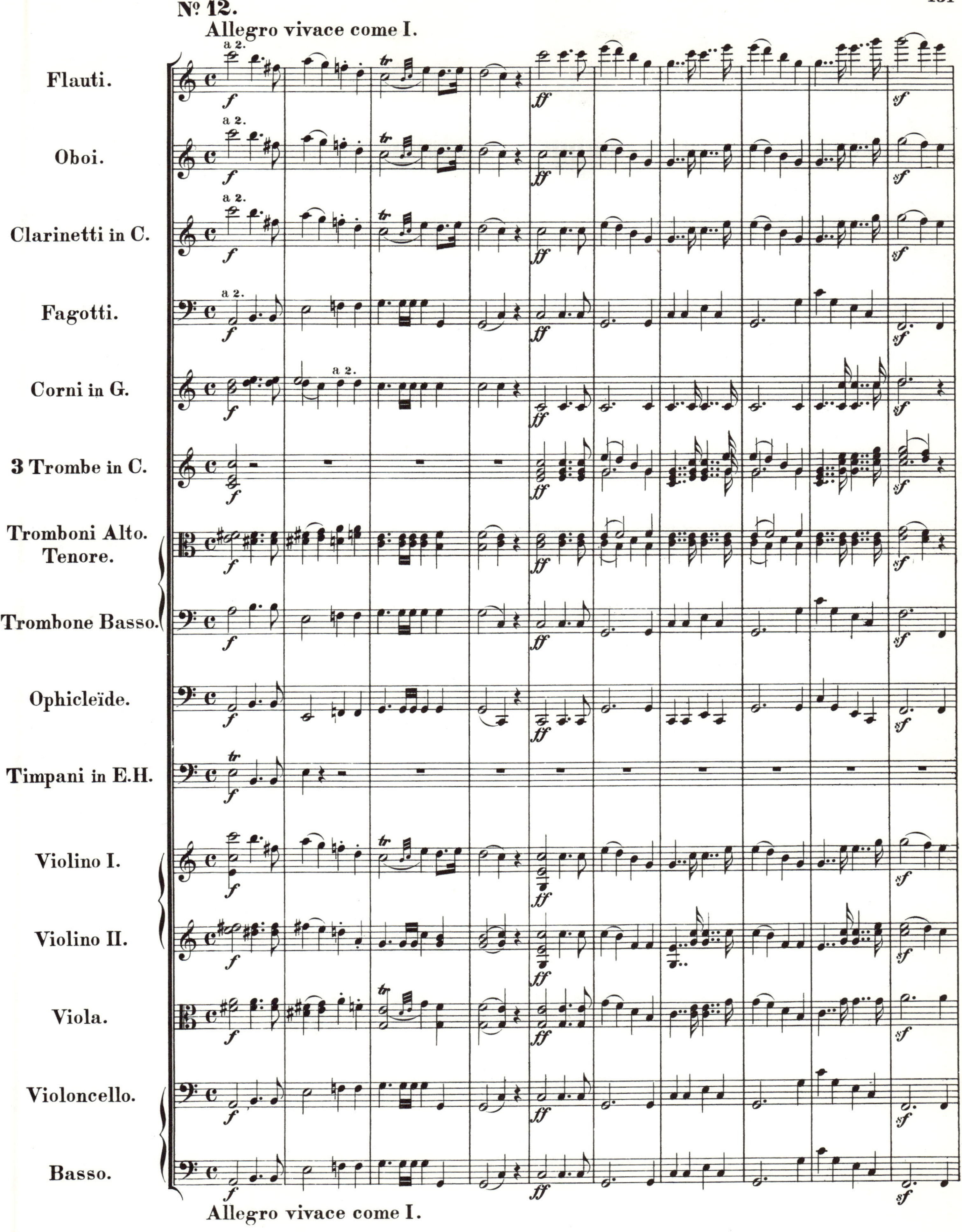
Nº 12.
Allegro vivace come I.
Flauti.
Oboi.
Clarinetti in C.
Fagotti.
Corni in G.
3 Trombe in C.
Tromboni Alto. Tenore.
Trombone Basso.
Ophicleïde.
Timpani in E.H.
Violino I.
Violino II.
Viola.
Violoncello.
Basso.
a 2.
tr
Allegro vivace come I.

a 2.
(Hier ist der Hochzeitszug fortgezogen
und es wird dunkel auf der Scene.)
(Exit the wedding procession and
it grows dusky on the scene.)

pp
pp
pp
pp
pp
Puck. Jetzt beheult der Wolf den Mond, pp. bis:
Keine Maus
Störe dies geweihte Haus!
Voran komm' ich mit Besenreis,
Den Flur zu fegen blank und weiss.
divisi
pp
divisi
pp
Puck. Now the hungry lion roars, etc. till:
Not a mouse
Shall disturb this hallow'd house.
I am sent, with broom, before,
To sweep the dust behind the door.
(Puck kommt.)
(Enter Puck.)
pizz.
pizz.

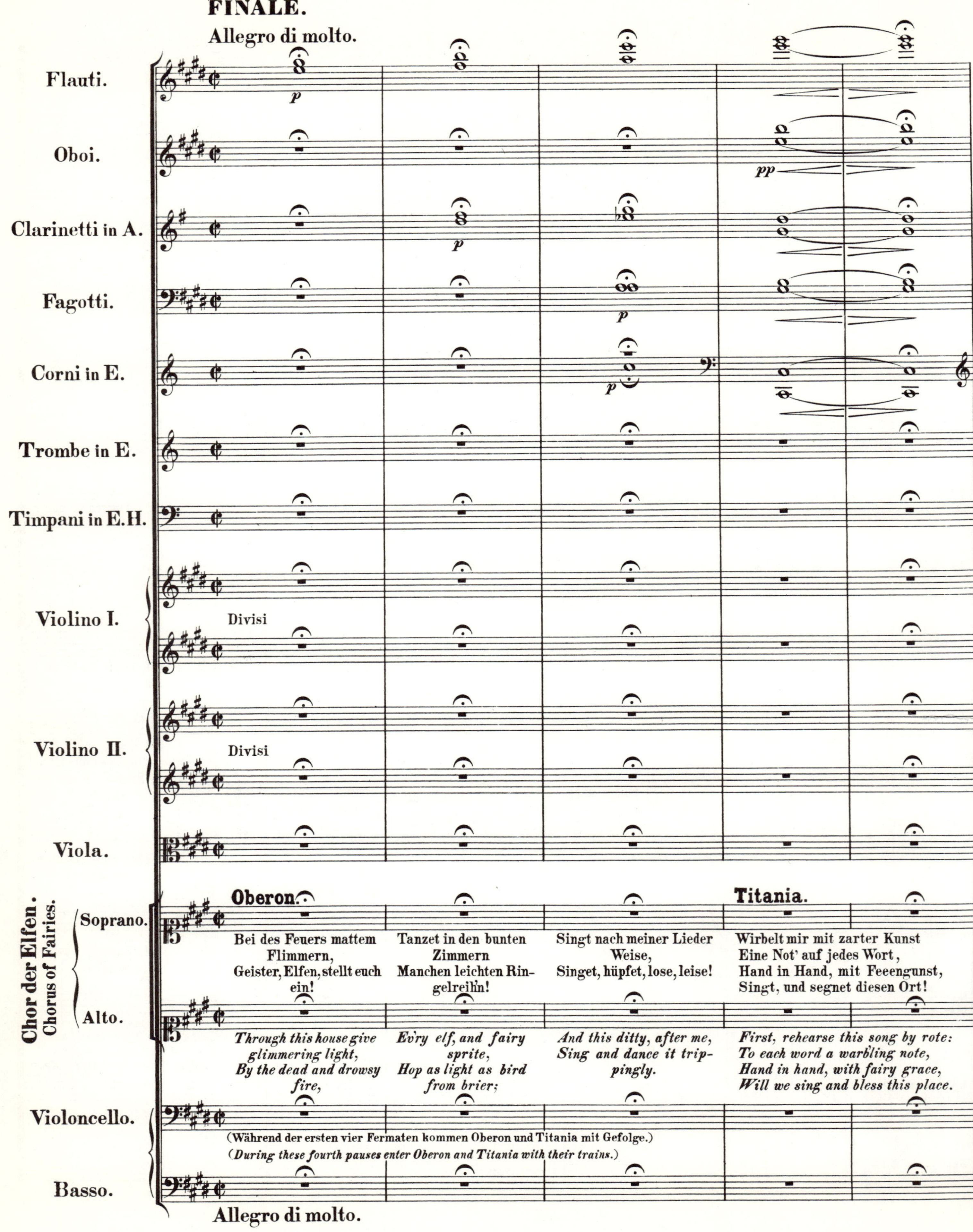
FINALE.
Allegro di molto.
Flauti.
Oboi.
Clarinetti in A.
Fagotti.
Corni in E.
Trombe in E.
Timpani in E.H.
Violino I.
Divisi
Violino II.
Divisi
Viola.
Chor der Elfen.
Chorus of Fairies.
Soprano.
Alto.
Oberon.
Titania.
Bei des Feuers mattem Flimmern, Geister, Elfen, stellt euch ein!
Tanzet in den bunten Zimmern Manchen leichten Ringelreih'n!
Singt nach meiner Lieder Weise, Singet, hüpfet, lose, leise!
Wirbelt mir mit zarter Kunst Eine Not' auf jedes Wort, Hand in Hand, mit Feeengunst, Singt, und segnet diesen Ort!
Through this house give glimmering light, By the dead and drowsy fire,
Ev'ry elf, and fairy sprite, Hop as light as bird from brier;
And this ditty, after me, Sing and dance it trippingly.
First, rehearse this song by rote: To each word a warbling note, Hand in hand, with fairy grace, Will we sing and bless this place.
Violoncello.
(Während der ersten vier Fermaten kommen Oberon und Titania mit Gefolge.)
(During these fourth pauses enter Oberon and Titania with their trains.)
Basso.
Allegro di molto.

pp
(Mit Tanz.) (With dance.)
Bei des Feu - ers mat - tem Flim - mern, Gei - ster, El - fen, stellt euch hin!
Tro' this house give glim' - ring light, by the dead and drow - si fire,
pizz.

pp
pizz.
pizz.
Tan - zet in den bun - ten Zim - mern man - chen leich - ten Rin - gel - reih'n! Singt nach
ev' - ry elf and fai - ry sprite hop as light as bird from brier. And this

arco
pp
sei - ner Lie - der Wei - se, sin - get, hü - pfet, lo - se, lei - se! Bei des Feu - ers
dit - ty, and this dit - ty, and this dit - ty, af - ter me, sing and dance it

pizz.
pizz.
mat - tem Flim - mern, Gei - ster, El - fen, stellt euch ein! Singt nach sei - ner Lie - der
trip - ping - ly, sing and dance it trip - ping - ly. And this dit - ty, and this

pp
pp
pp
arco
Wei - se, sin - get, hü - pfet, lo - se, lei - se! Bei des Feu - ers mat - tem Flim - mern,
dit - ty, and this dit - ty, af - ter me, sing and dance it trip - ping - ly,

tr
arco
pp
p
Gei - ster, El - fen, stellt euch ein, lei - - - se, lei - se stellt euch ein!
sing and dance it trip - ping - ly, sing and dance i trip - ping - ly.
arco
pizz.
a 2.

pizz.

pizz.

pizz.

pizz.

Viole

SOLO. I^ter^ Elfe. (1. Fairy.)

Wir - belt mir mit zar - ter Kunst ei - ne Not' auf je - des Wort, Hand in

First, re - hearse the song by rote: to each word a warb - ling note, hand in

Vclli

Viola.
TUTTI.
Hand, mit Fee - en - gunst, singt und seg - net die - sen Ort!
hand, with fai - ry grace, will we sing and bless this place.
Singt und seg - net die - sen
Will we sing and bless this
TUTTI.
Singt und seg - net die - sen
Will we sing and bless this

Viol. I.
Viol. II.
pizz.
arco
Viole
pizz.
arco
SOLO.
Ort! Hand in Hand, mit Fee - en - gunst, singt und seg - net die - sen Ort, Hand in Hand, mit Fee - en -
place. Hand in hand, with fai - ry grace, we will sing and bless this place, hand in hand, with fai - ry
Ort!
place.
pizz.
arco

gunst, singt und seg-net die-sen Ort, Hand in Hand, mit Fee-en-gunst, singt
grace, we will sing and bless this place, hand in hand, with fai-ry grace, we
pp
p
p
p
p
Vcl.
Basso
divisi
pizz.
sf

pizz.
arco
pizz.
pizz.
arco
pizz.
und seg_net die_sen Ort, singt, und seg_ net, und seg_ net, und seg_net die_ sen
will sing and bless this place, we will sing, will sing, will sing and bless this
arco
pizz.

pp
pp
pp
a 2.
pp
pp
arco
arco
arco
arco
pizz.
Viola.
arco
Tutti.
Ort!
place.
Bei des Feu-ers mat-tem Flim-mern, Gei-ster, El-fen, stellt euch ein! Tan-zet
Tutti.
Thro' this house give glim'-ring light, by the dead and drow-sy fire: Ev'-ry
arco
Velli.
arco

pp
pp
pp
pp
pp
arco
in den bun - ten Zim - mern man - chen leich - ten Rin - gel - reih'n! Singt nach
elf, and fai - ry sprite, hop as light as bird from brier. And this

a 2.
a 2.
a 2
a 2.
sempre pp
a 2.
sempre pp
a 2.
sempre pp
sempre pp
sempre pp
sempre pp
Viol. II.
sempre pp
pizz.
sei - ner Lie - der Wei - se, sin - get, hü-pfet, lo - se, lei-se, lo - se, lei - se,
dit - ty, af - ter me, sing and dance it trip - ping - ly, sing and dance it,
sei - ner Lie - der Wei - se, sin - get, hü-pfet, lo - se, lei - se, lo - se, lei - se,
dit - ty, af - ter me, sing and dance it trip - ping - ly, sing and dance it,
pizz.
pizz.
sempre pp

a 2.
pp
a 2.
pp
pp
a 2.
pp
pp
pp
pizz.
arco
pp
pizz.
arco
pizz.
arco
pp
pizz.
arco
pizz.
arco
pp
pizz.
arco
Viol. II.
pizz.
arco
pp
pizz.
arco
arco
pizz.
p
lo - se, lei - - se, lo - se, lei - se, lo - se, lei - - se, lo - se, lei -
sing and dance it, sing and dance it, sing and dance it, sing and dance
lei - - se, lo - se, lei - se, lei - - se,
dance it, sing and dance it, dance it,
Vel.
arco
pp
pizz.
arco
pp
Basso
arco
pp
pizz.
arco
pp

Un poco ritard.
pp
pp
pp
pp
pp
pizz.
Oberon.
Nun bis Tages Wieder-kehr,
Elfen, schwärmt im Haus' umher!
Kommt zum besten Brautbett hin, Dass es Heil durch uns gewinn! Das Geschlecht,
se!
it!
Oberon.
Now, until the break of day,
Through this house each fairy stray.
Tho the best bride-bed will we, which by us shall blessed be; And the issue,
p
lo - se, lei - - - se!
sing and dance it!
pizz.
pizz.
Un poco ritard.

dim.
dim.
dolce
pp
dim.
pp
pp
entsprossen dort, Sei gesegnet immerfort; Jedes dieser Paare sei Ewiglich im Lieben treu; Ihr Geschlecht soll nimmer schänden die Natur mit Feindes Händen; Und mit Zeichen
there create; Ever shall be fortunate. So shall all the couples three Ever true in loving be; And the blots of nature's hand Shall not in their issue stand; Never mole, hare-lip,

Viol. I.
Viol. II.
pp
pp
pizz.
pizz.
schlimmer Art,
Muttermaal und Hasenschart;
Werde durch des Himmels Zorn Ihnen nie ein Kind gebor'n_
Elfen, sprengt durch's ganze Haus Tropfen heil'gen Wiesenthau's, Jedes Zimmer, jeden Saal
nor scar,
Nor mark prodi_gious, such as are
Despised in nativity, Shall upon their chil_dren be._
With this field_dew consecrate,
Ever fairy take his gait!
And each several chamber bless,

a Tempo I. Allegro molto.
a 2.
p
dolce
p
dolce
pp
3
3
pp
arco
p
pp
weiht und segnet all - zumal! Friede sei in diesem Schloss, und sein Herr ein Glücksgenoss!
Nun genung, fort im Sprung, Trefft mich in der Dämmerung!
Through this palace, with sweet peace: E'er shall it in safety rest, And the owner of it blest.
Trip away; Make no stay; Meet me all by break of day.
p
Nun genung, fort im Sprung, trefft ihn
p
Trip a-way; make no stay; meet him
arco
p
arco
p
a Tempo I. Allegro molto.

Die Fermate wird immer fort gehalten so lange Puck spricht, bis:
in der Däm-me-rung!
Puck.
Wenn wir Schatten euch beleidigt,
So verheisst auf Kobolds Ehren
alsdann gleich die Flöten auf dem Wort,
Puck, dass wir Euch Dank gewähren: Ist ein Schelm zu heissen willig,
Wenn dies nicht geschieht, wie billig. Nun gute Nacht!
Das Spiel zu enden, Begrüsst uns mit gewognen Händen!
all by break of day.
Puck.
If we shadows have offended, etc. till:
And, as I'm an honest Puck,
(The flutes fall in with the word.)
If we have unearned luck
Now to 'scape the serpent's tongue,
We will make amends, ere long:
Else the Puck a liar call.
So, good night unto you all.
Give me your hands, if we be friends,
And Robin shall restore amends.
(Oberon, Titania und Gefolge ab.)
(Exeunt Oberon, Titania and Train.)
tr
pp

The Hebrides Overture, or Fingal's Cave, Op. 26

Dedicated to the Crown Prince of Prussia (later King Frederick William IV)

Allegro moderato.

Flauto I.
Flauto II.
Oboe I.
Oboe II.
Clarinetto I in A.
Clarinetto II in A.
Fagotto I.
Fagotto II.
Corni in D.
Trombe in D.
Timpani in H. Fis.
Violino I.
Violino II.
Viola.
Violoncello.
Basso.

p
f
dim.
sf dim.
pp
tr

f
sf
pp
f
sf
pp
f
sf
pp
f
sf
pp
f
sf
pp
f
pp
f
pp
II.
I
pp
tr
f
f
sf cresc.
ff
sf dim.
pp
f
cresc.
ff
dim.
pp
f
cresc.
ff
dim.
pp
f
cresc.
ff
dim.
pp
f
cresc.
ff
dim.

p
sf
p
sf
tr
pp

mf cresc.
mf cresc.
mf cresc.
mf cresc.
p
ff
p
p
ff
ff
p
ff
pp
ff
pp
pp
ff
tr
pp
ff
pp
p
ff
pp
p
ff
pp
p
ff
pp
ff
pp
ff
pp

A
dim.
dim.
tr
a 2
dim.
dim.
A

pp
pp
cresc.
p
cresc.
pp
cre
dol.
dim.
pp
cre
dol.
dim.
pp
cre
p
p
dim.
pp
cre
p
p
dim.
pp
cre
p
p
dim.
pp
cre

B
cresc.
ff
sf
mf
scen
do
f non legato
f
B

ff
ff
ff
ff
ff
ff
ff
ff
tr
tr

sf
f
sf sf sf
sf sf
ff
tr

C
tr
sf
ff
sf
dim.
ff
sf
dim.
sf
p
p
p
p
C

ff
sf
dim.
f
ff marcato
marcato
mf
pp
p

f
dim.
p
f con forza
f con forza
f
f
f con forza
f
f con forza
f
f
f
f con forza
f
f
f
f con forza
f
f
f con forza
f
f
f con forza
f
f
sf
mf marcato
sempre pp
sempre pp
sempre pp
sempre pp

D
f
p
cresc.
dim.
D

cresc.
f
dim.
pp stacc.
cresc.
f
pp stacc.
p
p
cresc.
f
pp stacc.
p
cresc.
f
pp stacc.
p
f
pp stacc.
p
f
pp stacc.
f
pp
cresc.
f
tr
pp
cresc.
f
p
cresc.
sf
sf
f
dim.
pp stacc.
p
cresc.
sf
sf
f
dim.
pp stacc.
f
pp stacc.
f
p
pp stacc.
f
p
pp stacc.

e leggiero
sempre pp
poco
a
poco
p
pizz.
sempre pp

cresc.
sempre cre - - - scen - - -
cresc.sempre
arco
p
cre - - - scen - - - do
sempre cre - - scen - - -

E
do
f
f
do
f
cresc.
cresc.
cresc.
cresc.
tr
non legato
E

ff con forza
ff con forza
f
f
ff con forza
f
f
ff con forza
f
ff
f
ff
f
f
ff
f
f
ff
f
ff con forza
ff
più f
sf sf sf sf
ff
più f
sf sf sf sf
ff
più f
sf sf sf sf
ff
più f
sf sf sf sf
ff non legato
più f
sf sf sf sf
ff non legato

ff
ff
ff
ff
ff
ff
ff
ff
f
ff
f
ff
tr
f
tr
ff
sf
sf
ff
sf
sf
ff
sf
sf
ff
sf
sf
ff
sf
sf
ff

F

f sf sf dim. p dim. pp p tranquillo

F

p
sf

p
dim.
sf
cresc.
sf
cresc.
sf
cre - scen - do
f
dim.
p
dim.
sf
cre - scen - do
f
dim.
p
dim.
sf
cre - scen - do
f
dim.
p
dim.
cre - scen - do
sf
sf
sf
sf
f
dim.
p
dim.
cre - scen - do
sf
sf
sf
sf
f
dim.
p
dim.

tranquillo assai
pp
p
p
dol.
p
p
dol.
pp
pp
pp
pp
div.
pp
pp
pp
pp
pp
pp
pp

Animato.
in tempo
Animato.
p stacc.
cresc.
p cresc.
dim.
un poco rit.
dim.
in tempo
dim.
un poco rit.
dim.
cresc.
Animato.
sf
pp
in tempo
stacc.
stacc.
un poco rit.
dim.
pizz.
Animato.
pizz.
un poco rit.
dim.
in tempo

cresc.
cresc.
cresc.
cresc.
stacc. cresc.
stacc. cresc.
p
f
p
f
cresc.
f
cresc.
cresc.
f
cresc.
stacc.
cresc.
p
cresc.
cresc.
cresc.
sf
cresc.
sf
cresc.
cresc.
sf
sf
cresc.
sf
cresc.
sf
arco
cresc.
sf
cresc.

G
ff
f
ff non legato
sf
arco
G ff non legato

ff
ff
ff
ff
ff
ff
ff
ff
f
f
tr
f
ff
ff
ff
ff
ff

tr
tr
f
f
f

H
f
con fuoco
ff
H

f
f
f
f
f
f
f
f

sf
sf
sf
sf
sf
sf
sf
sf
sf
sf
sf
sf

I
ff
sf
tr
I

p
dim.
pp
ff
pp
ff
pp
p
dim.
pp
ff
ff
ff
ff
ff
ff
ff
pp
ff
ff
pp
pizz.
ff
ff
pp
pizz.
ff
ff
pp
pizz.
ff
ff
pp
pizz.
ff
ff
pp
pizz.
ff
ff
pp

Calm Sea and Prosperous Voyage Overture, Op. 27

Dedicated to the Crown Prince of Prussia (later King Frederick William IV)

pp
p
pp
p
a 2.
espress.
p sf
dim.
sempre p
p dim.

p legg.
sf
f
dim.
p cresc.
p dim.
p
pp
sempre pp
dim.

Prosperous Voyage

Molto Allegro e vivace.

dim.
dim.
dim.
dim.
dim.
dim.
dim.
p cresc.
cresc.
cresc.
cresc.
cresc.
sf
sf
p

p
cresc.
sempre cresc.
sf
p
sf
p
cresc.
sempre cresc.
sf
p
sf
p
cresc.
sempre cresc.
sf
p
cresc.
sempre cresc.
p
cresc.
sempre cresc.
p
cresc.
sempre cresc.
p
cresc.
sf
sf
p
p
cresc.
sempre cresc.
p
sf
p
sf
sf
p
sf
cresc.
p
p
cresc.
p
p
sempre cresc.
p

sf
p
mf
molto cresc.
cresc.
sempre

f
ff
cresc.
tr
al

A
p
leggiero
p
leggiero
pp
p
leggiero
p
leggiero
pp
leggiero
pp
leggiero
pp
ff
pp
ff
pp
ff
pp
pizz.
ff
p
pizz.
ff
p
pizz.
ff
p
pizz.
ff
p
pizz.
ff
p
A

pp
mf
arco
f marcato
sf
fpp
p

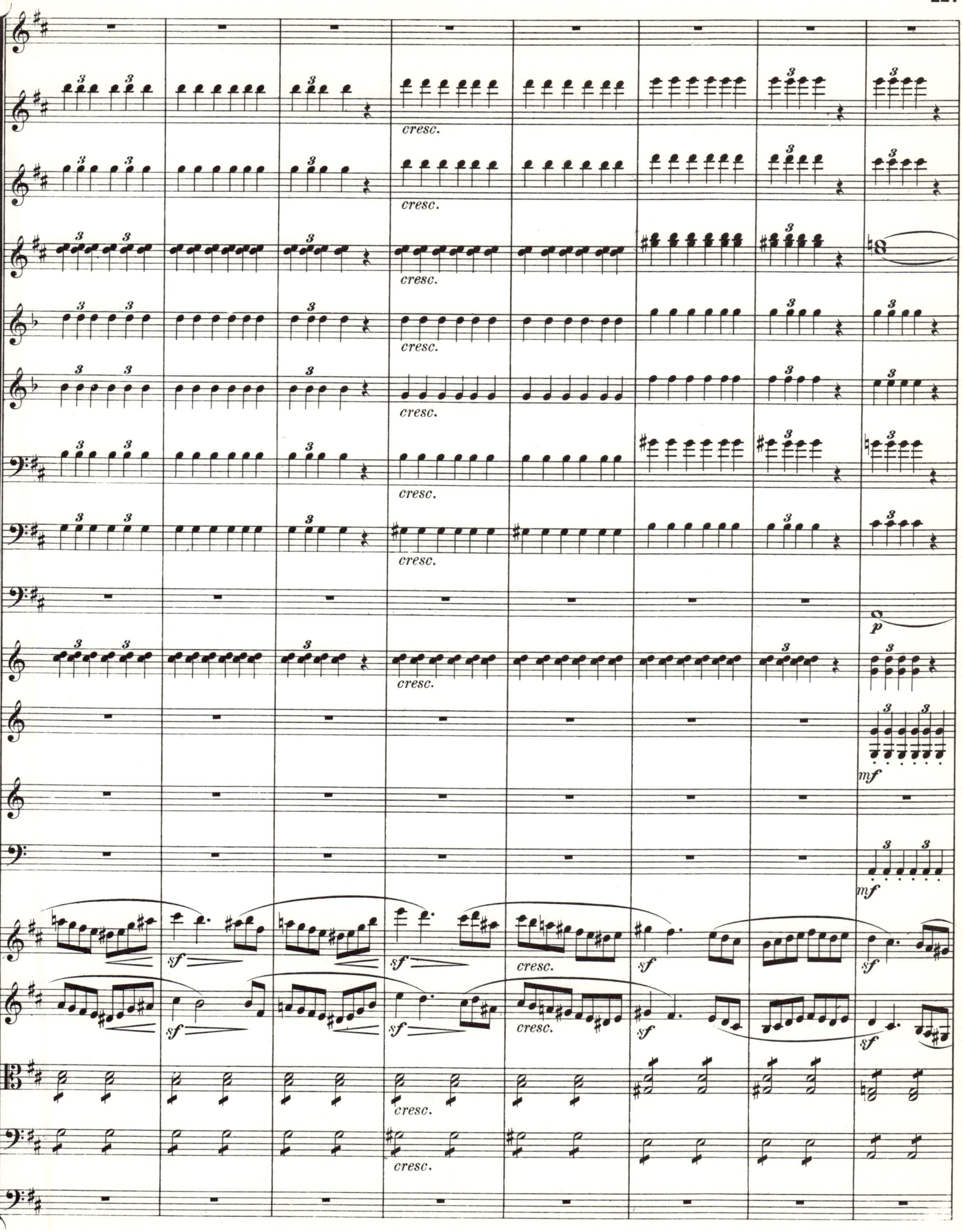
cresc.
sf
cresc.
p
mf

B
cresc.
f
ff
B

tr
f
marcato
a 2.
f marcato
f marcato
a 2.
f
f
f marcato
f marcato
f marcato

C
C

sf
sf
f
f
f
sf
sf
sf

D
a 2.
D

p
pp
dim.
f
sf
sf
dolce

mf
p
dim.
pp

sf
dim.
p
sf
dim.
p
espress.
sf
dim.
p
dim.
p
sf
dim.
p
dim.
dim.
p
dim.
dim.
p
dim.
dim.
pp
pp
p
p
p
pp
p
p
p
sf
p
sf
p
p

a 2.
cresc.
f
p
pp
tr

cresc.
f
a 2.
tr
p cresc.
sf

E
cresc.
sf
cresc.
più f
marcato
ff
E

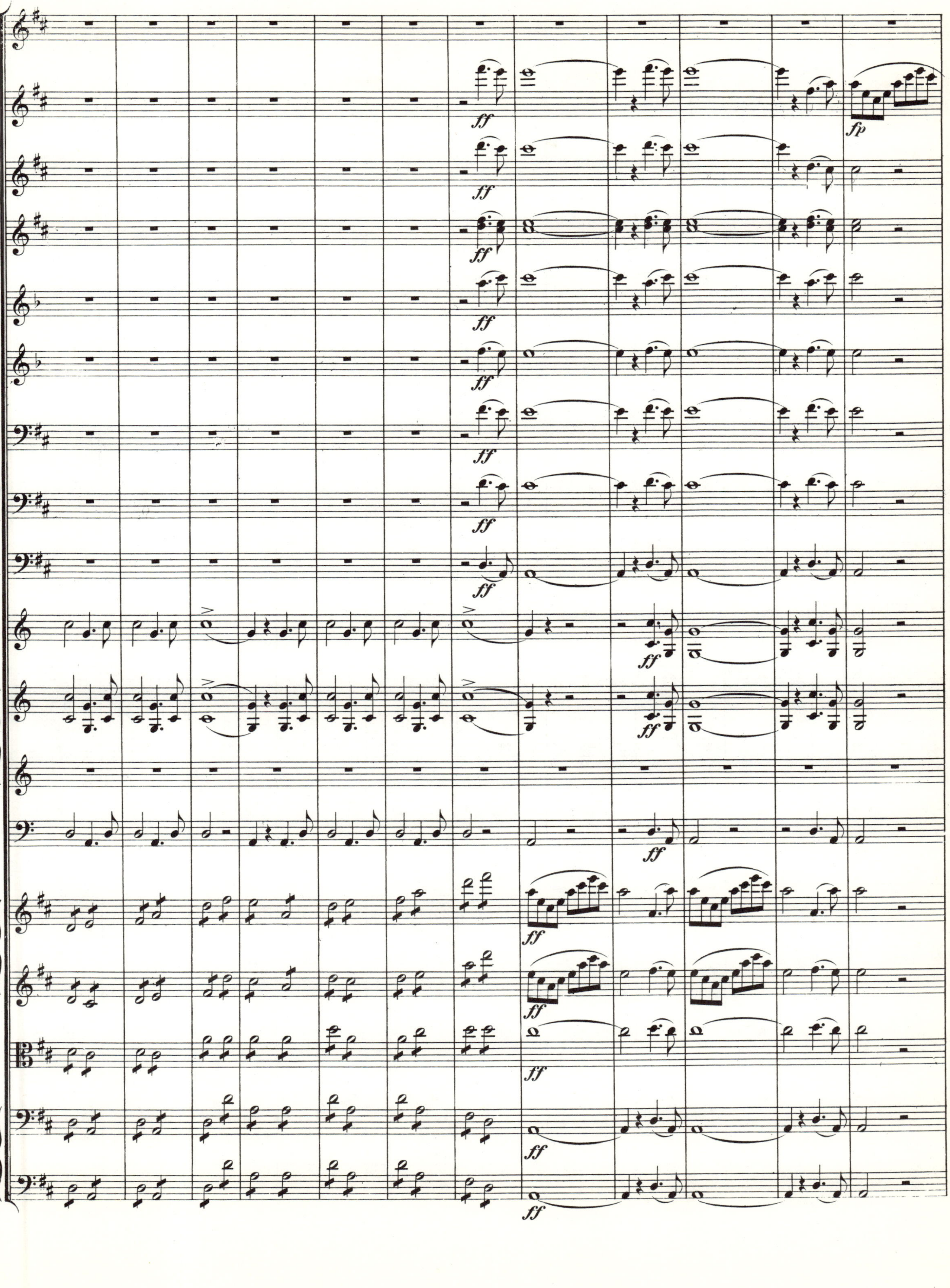
ff
fp

dim.
p
dim.
pp
dim.
pp
dim.
pp
pizz.
dim.
pp
pizz.
dim.
dim.
pp
dim.
dim.
pp
a 2.
p dim.
pp
pizz.
p dim.
pp

p
pp

F
mf
mf
p
p
p
p
p
p marcato
p marcato
mf
pp
pp
p
p
p
sf
F p
sf

cresc.
sf
p
tr

f
f
f
f
f
f
f
f
f
f
p
f
p
p
f
p
f
sf
f
sf
sf
sf
sf
sf

G
ff
sf
f
cresc.
mf
dim.
più f
ff dim.
tr
sf
f cresc.
G ff

legg.
pp
pp
pp
pp
p dim.
pp
p dim.
tr
pp
dim.
p
dim.
p
p dim.
pp
sf
p
p dim.
pp

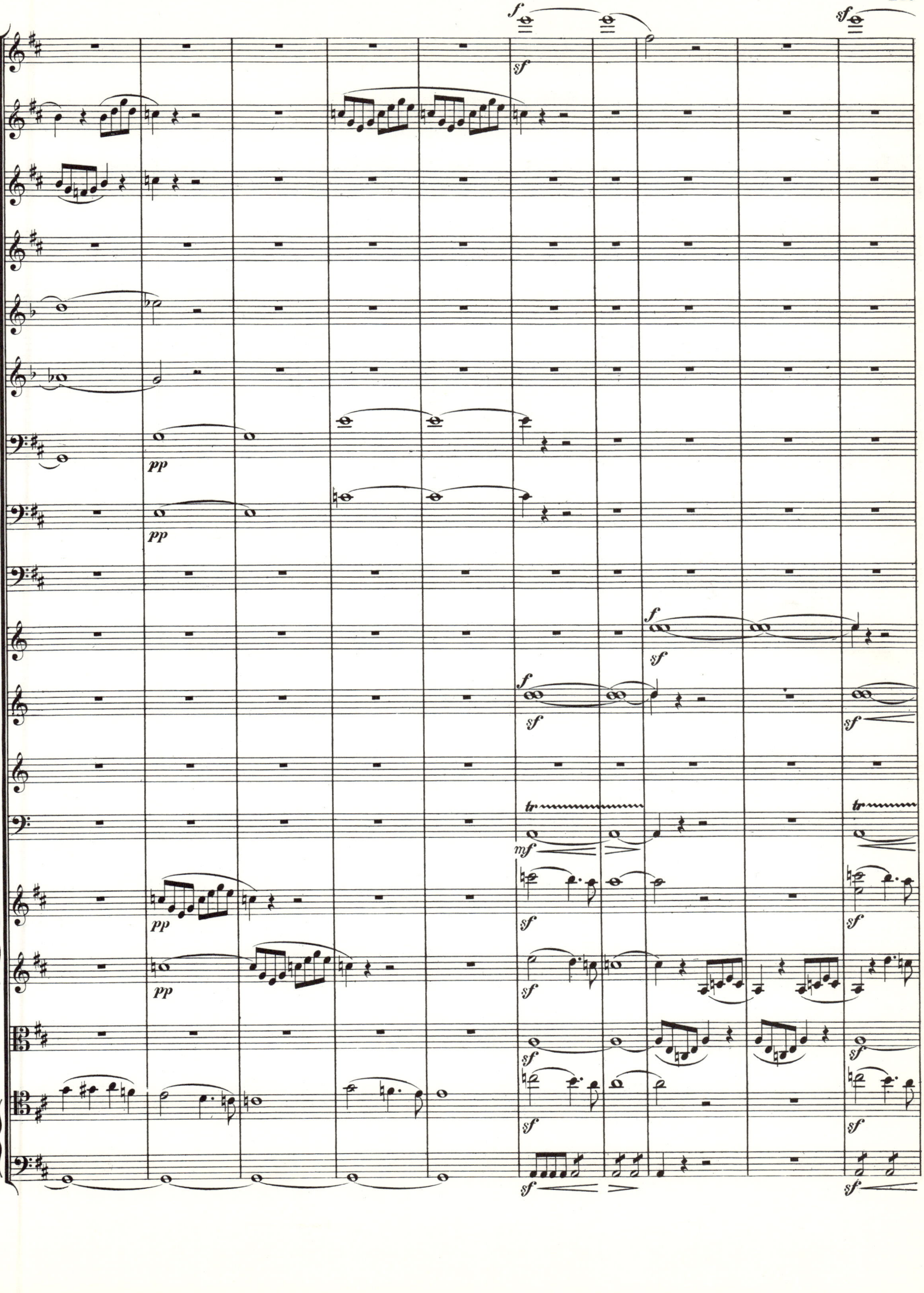
f
sf
pp
pp
f
sf
f
sf
tr
mf
sf
pp
sf
pp
sf
sf
sf
sf
sf
sf
sf

sf
tr
cresc.
sf
sempre cresc.
f
più f
cresc.
sempre cresc.
f
più f
cresc.
sempre cresc.
f
più f
cresc.
sempre cresc.
sf
f
sf
sf
più f
sempre cresc.
f
sf
sf
più f

H
ff
sf
f
H

legg.
legg.
espress.

p
pp
p
pp
p
p
p
p
p>
pp
pp
pp
p
pp
pp
p
pp
pp
p
pp
p
pp

tr
tr
tr
pp
pp
sempre p
cresc.
sf
sf
pp
sempre p
cresc.
sf
sf
pp
cresc.
sf
sf
pp
cresc.
sf
sf
pp
cresc.
sf
sf
p
p
p
p
p
p
p

p
cresc.
mf

cresc.
p
cresc.
p
cresc.
cresc.
cresc.
cresc.
cresc.
cresc.
cresc.
cresc.
cresc.
sf
cresc.
sf
cresc.
sf
cresc.

I
ff
ff
a 2
ff
cresc.
f
mf
tr
I

f
ff
sf
mf
cresc.

ff
sf
f
mf
più f

cresc.
f
sempre più f - - - - - al - ff
più f
più f

Allegro maestoso. Dasselbe Tempo, die Achtel wie vorher die Viertel.*

* Same tempo, the eighth notes like the preceding fourth notes.

ten. assai

tr

ten. assai

ten. assai

ff
sf
ffp
dim.
pp
tr

Symphony No. 3 in A ("Scottish"), Op. 56

Dedicated to Queen Victoria of England

Die einzelnen Sätze dieser Symphonie müssen gleich auf einander folgen, und nicht durch die sonst gewöhnlichen längeren Unterbrechungen von einander getrennt werden. Für die Hörer kann der Inhalt der einzelnen Sätze auf dem Programm des Concertes angegeben werden wie folgt: *

Introduction und Allegro agitato.— Scherzo assai vivace.— Adagio cantabile.— Allegro guerriero und Finale maestoso.

* The movements of this symphony must follow one another immediately, and must not be separated by the customary long pauses. For the listeners, the content of the movements can be indicated on the concert program as follows:

al
ff
sf
dim.
p
trem.
pp
pizz.

Allegro un poco agitato. ♩.= 100.
ten.
ten.
ten.
dim.
p
dim.
pp
sempre pp
arco
arco

p
cresc.
pp
a 2.
sf
sempre più cresc.
sf
al

Assai animato ♩.=120.

a 2.
a 2.
C
mf
pp
p
pizz.
pizz.
cresc.
cantabile
arco
arco

espress.
p
sf
pp
dim.
p cresc.
cresc.
a 2.
D
f
tr
pp
cresc.

cresc.
piú f
ff
a 2
sf
E
p
f
fp

1.
2.
pp
p
a 2.
pp sempre
cresc.

F
f cresc.
ff
cresc.
f
sf
p
cantabile
mf
cre
scen
do
dim.
sce
F

p
p
espress.
cresc.
cre
scen
do
cresc.
cre
scen
do
cre
scen
do
cre
scen
do
cre
scen
do
G
cresc.
f
sf
dim.
dim.
p
cresc.
G

f
sf
tr
più f
ff

a 2.
ff
a 2.
ff
a 2.
ff
a 2.
ff
sf
sf
sf
sf
sf
sf
sf
tr
sf
ff
ff
ff
ff
ff
ff
ff
ff
ff
sf
sf
sf
sf
sf
H
p
p
p
p
p
pp
pp
pp
p
p
p
p
p
p
p
fp
fp
H

dim.
dim.
dim.
p
p
p
p
dim.
dim.
pp
pp
dim.
p
dim.
dim.
p
dim.
dim.
p
dim.
dim.
pizz.
dim.
dim.
pizz.
dim.
dim.
pp
pp
p
p
pp
pp
pp
arco
p cantabile
sf
p
pp

K
a 2.
a 2.
sf
p
cresc.
sf
mf
tr
cresc.
pp cre - - scen - - do
f
K
più f
ff

L
a 2.
p
sf
fp
pp
dim.

dim.
dim.
dim.
dim.
pp
pp
dim.
pp
dim.
dim.
dim.
pp
pp
pp
pp
M
p
cresc.
p
cresc.
a 2.
cresc.
p
cresc.
p
cresc.
cresc.
p
pp
sempre pp
pp
pp
sempre pp
pp
pp
sempre pp
pp
pp
sempre pp
pp
pp
sempre pp
pp
M

p
cresc.
sempre
dim.
fz
sf
ff
a 2.
tr
f

N
ff
dim.
p
cresc.
sf
fff
f
tr

O Assai animato.
O

a 2.
P
dim.
p
f
ff
Andante come I. 𝅗𝅥 = 72.
pp
sf
dim.
pizz.
attacca

Vivace non troppo. ♩=126.

a 2.

a 2.

in B.

p

a 2.

f

sf

in F.

a 2.

in F C.

arco

pp

cresc. dim.

pp

sempre assai leggiero staccato

arco

pp

cresc. dim.

pp

sempre assai leggiero staccato

arco

pp

cresc. dim.

pp sempre assai leggiero staccato

f

sempre pp

sempre pp

sempre pp

pizz.

A
a 2.
a 2.
mf
dim.
f
cresc.
p
dim.
arco
pizz
p
A
cresc.
a 2.
sf
pizz.

cresc.
cresc.
cresc.
a 2.
ff
al
arco
arco
sf
più f
f

B
sf
sf
sf
sf
dim.
pp
pp
dim.
pp
p
pp
p
pp
B
pp
sf
p
pp
pp
pp
pp
pp
pp

C
sf
p
pp
a 2.
dim.
mf
p
pizz.
arco

a 2.
cresc.
p
f
fsf
arco
p cresc.
ff
a 2.
p

D
p
p
sf
p
cresc.
cresc.
fpp
fpp
p
cresc.
p
cresc.
p
cresc.
p
p
cresc.
pizz.
cresc.
p
pizz.
cresc.
pizz.
p
cresc.
D
p
p
p
p
p
p
arco
p
arco
p
arco
p
p

E
cresc.
f
ff
p
tr
sempre p
pp

p
dim.
cresc.
sf
f
a 2.
mf cresc.
pp
p cresc.

F
a 2.
a 2.
a 2.
a 2.
a 2.
a 2.
a 2.
p cresc.
F

a 2.
sf
a 2.
sf
a 2.
sf
ff
ff
tr

G
sempre ff
ff
G
p
leggiero
dim.
pizz.

a 2.
arco
arco
dim.
dimin.
sempre dim.
p sempre, dim.

H
pp
pp
pp
pp
pp
pp
cresc.
dim.
pp
pp
H pp
pp
p
pp
pp
I
p
pp
pp
pp
pp
pp
pp
pizz.
pizz.
pizz.
pizz.
pizz.
pp
attacca

Adagio. ♪=76.
in A.
cresc.
in D.
in A.E.
arco
pizz.
p cresc.
dim.
cantabile
divisi
pp sempre pizz.
A

p cresc.
f
pp
p
cresc.
arco
sf

B
a 2.
cresc.
p
sf
f
B
ff
sf
più f
C
tr
trem.
a 2.
C

p
cresc.
dim.
f
pizz.
a 2.
arco
tr
pp
mf
sf
p cresc.

D
cresc.
arco
a 2.
tr
p
f
ff

dim.
p
cantabile
pp
p
sf
pizz.
cantabile e marcato
dim.

sempre pp
sempre pp
cresc.
cresc.
sf
sf
cresc..
cresc..
cresc.
cresc.
cresc.
cresc.
cresc.
dim..
dim..
p
sf
dim.
sf
dim.
dim.
sf
p
pp
pp
sf
dim.
p
p
p
f
dim.
f
dim.
f
dim.
f
dim.
f
dim.
p
arco
arco
p
p
p
arco

E
dim.
a 2.
pp
p
cresc.
f
sf
trem.
ff
p cresc.
tr

F
più f
a 2.
ff
dim.
ben tenuto
p
cresc.
pp
F

Allegro vivacissimo. 𝅗𝅥 = 126.
in C
ff
p
f p
cresc.
stacc.
sf

cresc.

A
a 2.
ff
tr
sf
A
a 2.

B
a 2.
a 2.
a 2.
a 2.
a 2.
a 2.
B
a 2.
a 2.

C

a 2.

a 2.

C

pizz.

pizz.

sf
p
pp
ff
arco
tr
cresc.
D
f
fp

cresc.
f
sf
p
fp
ff
tr

a 2.
marcato
E

sf
p
pp
pp
p
p
p
sf
pizz.
p
pizz.
p
sempre p
sempre p
cresc.
p
cresc.
p
cresc.
cresc.
cresc.
sf
p
sf
p
cresc.
sf
p
sf
p
cresc.
p
p
cresc.
p
p
cresc.
p
cresc.
p

p
p
dim.
dim.
dim.
arco
arco
dim.
dim.
cresc.
cresc.
dim.
dim.
F
p
p
pp
pp
pp
pp
F pp

p
p
pp
pp
pp
cresc.
cresc.
cresc.
p
p
cresc.
cresc.
cresc.
p
p
cresc.
cresc.

G
cresc.
p cresc.
f
sf
più f

a 2.
a 2.
H
H

al
f
sf
p
cresc.
sf cresc.
a 2.
tr
L
f

a 2.
a 2.
a 2.
a 2.

M
sempre ff
a 2.
sf
ff
dim.

ten.
sf
p
dim.
pp
ppp

espress.
cresc.
cresc.
dim.
dim.
dim.
ppp
dim.
dim.
dim.
dim.
pp
pp
pp
pp
sempre pp
sempre pp
pp
pp
pp

Allegro maestoso assai. ♩ = 104.
marcato assai la melodia
mf
sf
in A.
marcato assai la melodia
in D.
tr
pp
divisi
a 2.
cresc.

p
cresc.
sf
tr
divisi
al -

ff
sf
a 2
tr

a 2.
a 2.
a 2.
a 2.

sf
ff
tr

sf
ff
tr

Symphony No. 4 in A ("Italian"), Op. 90

cresc.
p
cresc.
p
cresc.
p
cresc.
p
cresc.
sf
p
sfp
cresc.
sf
p
sfp
pizz.
cresc.
pizz.
cresc.
pizz.
cresc.
f
f
a 2.
f
f
f
f
f
f
sfp
p
sfp
p
arco
p
arco
p
arco
p

dim.
dim.
p
p
p
p stacc.
p stacc.
p stacc.
p
p
p
cresc.
cresc.
cresc.
cresc.
ff
ff
ff
ff
ff
ff
a 2.
mf
f
sf
cresc.
ff

a 2.
a 2.
a 2.
a 2.
sf
sf
sf
sf
tr
sf
sf
sf
sf
sf
sf
sf
sf
sf
sf
sf
sf
sf
sf
sf
sf
mf
sf stacc.
sf
sf stacc.
sf
ff
ff

ff
ff
ff
ff
ff
ff
tr
sf
stacc.
fpp
pp
f
sf
p
A

sempre stacc.
sempre pp e stacc.
pizz.
pizz.

p
p
p
cresc.
cresc.
cresc.
pp
cresc.
pp
cresc.
pp
cresc.
pp
cresc.
p
cresc.
arco
cresc.
arco
cresc.
mf
mf
mf
mf
cresc.
cresc.
cresc.
mf
cresc.
mf
cresc.
mf
mf
mf

cresc.
f
sf
p
pp
tr

B
cresc.
pizz.
arco
B

1.
sf
p
fp
fsf
pizz.
cresc.
al
f
div.
arco

1. 2

fp fp fp fp fp fp sf pizz. arco f sf pizz. f pizz. f p p p p p p p p p p pp pp pp pp

pp
pp
pp
pp
pp
p
p
p
sempre pp
sempre pp
sempre pp
sempre pp
sempre pp

cresc.
mf
f

sf
f
tr
a 2.
C
ff

ff
ff
ff
ff
f
ff
f
ff
f
ff
ff
ff
ff
ff

ff
f
sf
p

p
p
p
pp
cresc.
p
pp
pp
pp
pp
pp

cresc.
mf
cresc.
sf
f
sf
poco a poco cresc.
p cresc.
mf
cresc.
poco a poco cresc.
cresc.
mf
cresc.
poco a poco cresc.
mf
cresc.
f
poco a poco cresc.
mf
cresc.
f
D
f
sf
ff
f
sf
f
f
f
sf
sf
sf
sf
f
sf
sf
sf
f
sf
sf
sf
p
f
sf
p
D
p

cresc.
p
a 2.
mf
sf
cresc.
cresc.
p
p
p
sf
sf
sf
sf
p
sf
sf
sf
sf
sf
p
p
p
p
p
p
p
p

p
p
pp
mf
mf
pizz.
p
sf
sf

p
cresc.
mf
pizz.
arco
E
al
f
dim.
tr

dim.
pp
p
f

cresc. cresc. cresc. cresc.

p p p

p cresc. cresc. p cresc. cresc. cresc. f f cresc. cresc. f cresc. f cresc.

p cresc. cresc. f cresc. p cresc. cresc. f cresc. p cresc. cresc. f cresc.

p cresc. cresc. cresc. f cresc. p cresc. cresc. cresc. f cresc. cresc. cresc.

p cresc. cresc. f cresc. p cresc. cresc. f cresc.

Più animato poco a poco.
Più animato poco a poco.

F
fp
dim.
stacc.
p e leggiero
p
divisi
pizz.
ff
sempre stacc. e p

cresc.
p
mf
sempre cresc.
arco
f
ff
sf
tr

p
fp
sf
a 2.
cresc.
f
mf

Andante con moto.
Flauto I.
Flauto II.
Oboi.
Clarinetti in A.
Fagotti.
Corni in A.
Violino I.
Violino II.
Viola.
Violoncello.
Basso.
a 2.
sempre stacc. e p
sempre stacc. e p

p
cresc.
sf
p
p
cresc.
sf
p
p
cresc.
sf
p
sempre p
sempre p
p
p
p
p
cresc.
sf
p
p
cresc.
sf
p
p
p
p

A
tr
p
sf

p
sf
dim.
f
sfp
ff
a 2.
cresc.
cresc. sf
B
B

p
sfp
sf
a 2.
tr
sempre p
C
dim.
mf
pp

sf
p
f
dim.
mf
a 2.
tr

pp pp pp pp pp pp pp pp pp
dim. dim. dim.
pp pp
p dim. pp pizz.
p dim. pp pizz.

Con moto moderato.

Flauti.
Oboi.
Clarinetti in A.
Fagotti.
Corni in E.
Trombe in E.
Timpani in E.H.
Violino I.
Violino II.
Viola.
Violoncello.
Basso.

p p p p p

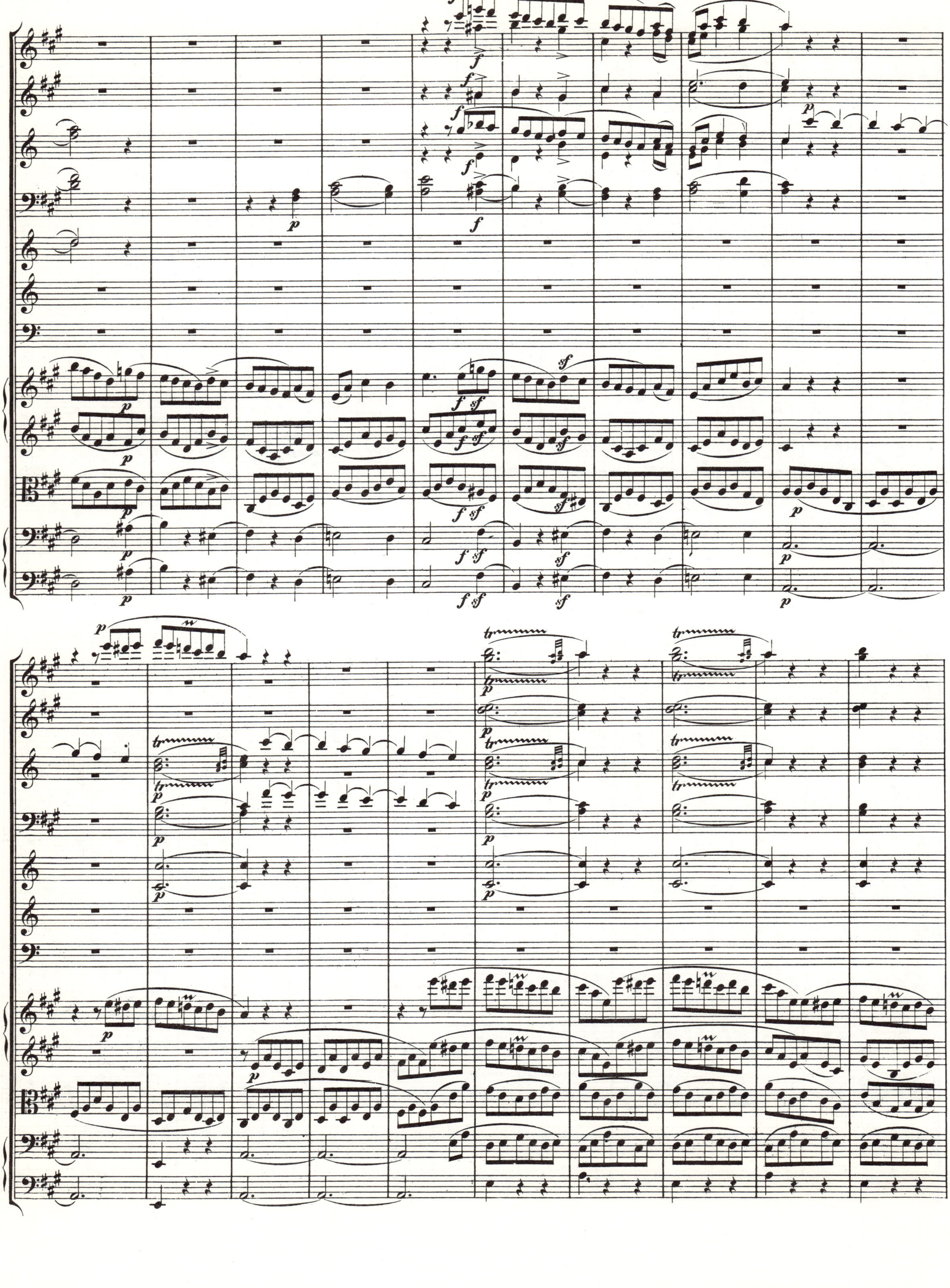

p cresc.
pp
p cresc.
p cresc.
p cresc.
p
p
dim.
pp
pizz.
p
dim.
pp
p
dim.
pp
pizz.
pp
p
dim.
pp
pizz.
pp
p
p
p
pp
cresc.
sf
p
cresc.
sf
p

mf
cresc.
arco
p
dol.
f
pp
tr

tr
cresc.
sf
p
cresc.
sf
p
p
pp
p
p
p
pizz.
arco
pizz.
arco
p
p
p
p
p
p
p
p
p

p
p
p
p
p
mf
p
p
p
p
p
cresc.
cresc.
cresc.
cresc.
cresc.
sf
sf
sf
f
dim.
sf
cresc.
sf
f
dim.
sf
f
cresc.
sf
f
dim.
sf
f
dim.
sf
f
dim.

p
f
cresc.
sf

p
p
tr
p
p
p
sf
sf
sf
sf
p
p
p
p
p
p
p cresc.
p cresc.
p cresc.
p cresc.
p
p
p

pp
p
pp
p
p
p
p
p
dim.
pp
p
pizz.
dim.
arco
dim.
pizz.
dim.
pp
arco
dim.
pizz.
pp
arco
p
pp
pp
pp
dim.
dim.
pp
tr
pp
p
dim.
pp
pizz.
pizz.
pp
pizz.
pp
pizz.
pp
pizz.
pp

SALTARELLO.

Presto.

p
pp
p
fp
p
p
p
cresc.
p
p
a 2.
pp
pp
pp
p
sf
sf
sf

cresc.
cresc. al
ff
p
tr
fsf

A
f
ff
p
p staccato
A
p

p
sf
pizz.

B
sf
a 2.
p legg.
sf
ff
dim.
p
B
p

p
pp
sf
dim.
tr

tr
p sempre
p
p

C

cresc.
f
a 2.

f
f
f
f
f f
f
f
f
f
ff
ff
ff
ff
ff
ff
ff
ff
ff
ff
ff
ff

ff
a 2.
p
f
dim.
D
fp

p
p
cresc.
mf
p cresc.
p
cresc.
cresc.
p
cresc.
f
cresc.
cresc.
f
cresc.
cresc.
f
cresc.
cresc.
cresc.
cresc.
cresc.

a 2.
f
f
ff
ff
ff
ff
ff
sempre cresc.
sempre cresc.
più f
più f
più f
più f
più f
sempre cresc.
sempre cresc.
sempre cresc.
sempre cresc.
sempre cresc.
tr
ff
ff
ff
ff
ff

a 2.
f
f
f
f
tr
tr
tr
f
f
f
f
E
sf
sf
sf
sf
sf
3
3
E

mf
dim.
p
f
dim.
pizz.
3

dim. pp dim. pp pp leggiero p pp pp pp pp pp pp

cresc. cresc. cresc. cresc. f p p pp cresc. f f f f f cresc. cresc. arco cresc. cresc. cresc. cresc. f f f f f